ALL THINGS HOLD TOGETHER
RECOVERING A CHRISTIAN WORLDVIEW

STEPHEN C. SHAFFER

ALL THINGS HOLD TOGETHER

Recovering Christian Worldview

Copyright © 2023 Stephen C. Shaffer. All rights reserved. Except for brief quotations in critical publications or reviews, no part of this book may be reproduced in any manner without prior written permission from the publisher. Write: Permissions, Peniel Press, 43 Stowe Terrace, Brantford, Ontario N3T 6P2 Canada or email: penielpress32@gmail.com

All Scripture quotations, unless otherwise indicated, are taken from the Holy Bible, New International Version, NIV. Copyright ©1973, 1978, 1984, 2011 by Biblica, Inc. Used by permission of Zondervan. All rights reserved worldwide. www.zondervan.com The NIV and New International Version are trademarks registered in the United States Patent and Trademark Office by Biblica, Inc.

Scripture citations marked (NRSV) are taken from the New Revised Standard Version Bible, copyright © 1989 National Council of the Churches of Christ in the United States of America. Used by permission. All rights reserved worldwide.

Scripture citations marked (NKJV) are taken from the New King James Version®. Copyright © 1982 by Thomas Nelson. Used by permission. All rights reserved.

Peniel Press

43 Stowe Terrace Brantford, ON N3T 6P2 Canada

www.penielpress.com

Cover design by Angie Koersen

PAPERBACK ISBN: 978-1-7779787-6-1

HARDCOVER ISBN: 978-1-7779787-5-4

EBOOK ISBN: 978-1-7779787-7-8

For my beloved, Olga,
a tree planted by streams of living water

CONTENTS

Introduction	vii
1. Made to Mend *Worldview in a Frayed World*	1
2. Flying Half a Ship *Knowledge in the Modern World*	19
3. It All Depends (On God) *Knowledge in a Christian Worldview*	41
4. Life Finds a Way *Change and Stability in the Modern World*	58
5. Certified Organic *Change and Stability in a Christian Worldview*	76
6. No Foundation *Morality in the Modern World*	91
7. Beauty Restored *Morality in a Christian Worldview*	111
Conclusion	128
Endnotes	139
Acknowledgments	147

INTRODUCTION

"He is before all things and in him all things hold together."
- Colossians 1:17

"I am for peace; but when I speak, they are for war."
- Psalm 120:7

Those who shout the loudest are often the most insecure. The father who has to raise his voice to tell his children, "I am your father; you need to listen to me!" may sound like he is full of authority, but likely feels his actual authority is quite fragile. It is not confidence, but insecurity, which causes him to raise his voice. The shrill voice (from the pulpit, on a podcast, or on a television screen) decrying the moral decay of the nation comes not from a place of confidence, but of fear. The person who posts the most audacious airbrushed and filtered photos on Instagram likely does so, not from self-confidence, but from insecurity. Those who shout the loudest are often the most insecure.

In the contemporary West, the loudest voices in the church are often the most insecure as well. This insecurity leads to a perpetual defensive posture toward the world around us. We feel assailed at every front. No rest, no quarter can be given. As the culture continues to move along certain paths, the church feels pushed further into the margins. Many double down on raising the alarm. This constant "state of alarm" changes how we live our faith in the world and how we disciple Christians to live faithfully in a fractured time. If we are at war, then what we need are weapons. Like citizens who defend their homeland with every spade, shovel, and pitchfork, we run the danger of taking implements that were meant to till the soil of faith and use them to combat our enemies.

Even if there are grave concerns about the age we inhabit, this war-like defensive posture damages the disciples of Jesus. At the very least, it creates a fragile faith that masks fear with bravado. At its worst, it undermines the witness of the church, as our pews and pulpits become filled with voices every bit as anxious and combative as the world around us.

All Things Hold Together is a call to turn away from the shrill voices screaming for a culture war, voices that proclaim confidence but instead hide a deep fear and insecurity about the future of the Christian faith. It is an invitation to return to an older, quieter, and more confident posture of Christian faith.

This is a book about the Christian worldview — quietly and confidently receiving the world as it truly is and not as we imagine it to be. But even Christian worldview has, at times, been taken up by those preparing for battle. It is a pruning hook that has been turned into a spear. It is a plowshare that has been molded into a sword.

So, in order to return to a more confident faith with a more humble and open posture, we must go back beyond the last few decades of common teaching on Christian worldview. We must return and draw from the well of a theologian named Herman Bavinck. But before we do that, we must first get clear on what exactly a "worldview" is and why we would want one.

WHAT DO WE MEAN BY A WORLDVIEW?

The term "worldview" or "Christian worldview" (and I will be using the two terms interchangeably) came into the English-speaking world largely through the work of Dutch theologians teaching in the United States after the turn of the 20th century. They were translating words and concepts that had been used extensively in Dutch (*wereldbeschouwing*) and German (*weltanschauung*) theology since the 19th century, but for which there was no ready word in English. Al Wolters lists a series of common synonyms for 'worldview,' including life perspective, confessional vision, principles/ideals, and system of values.[1] A worldview might be more accurately called a "world and life view." It involves viewing reality as it is.

In some sense, a Christian worldview is 'viewing the world from a Christian perspective.' However, on a deeper level, it is 'viewing things as they truly are.' The claim of a Christian worldview is that viewing the world from the perspective of the Christian faith actually matches the truth of the world as it is. Despite popular usage, worldview is not merely how each one of us — personally, from our perspective — views the world. It is instead a claim about how the world actually is, about how we should live in the world because of what it is, what it is for, where it came from, who we are, and where we are going (among other questions). Worldview is 'the true way the world works.'

In his book on Christian worldview entitled *Creation Regained*, Al Wolters identifies the Christian worldview as "the comprehensive framework of one's basic beliefs about things."[2] Each part of this definition is important. According to Wolters, a worldview is a framework of beliefs. By beliefs, he is not talking about opinions or feelings, but about a kind of knowledge. Beliefs can be supported and defended with arguments and are a claim about the way the world actually is. In particular, a worldview deals with committed beliefs, with convictions — those things we are willing to defend and for which we are willing to make sacrifices.

However, as Wolters notes, worldview is not simply a set of isolated and individual beliefs, but a 'comprehensive framework.' Even if people often hold contradictory beliefs, worldview is an attempt to be consistent and to see how all one's beliefs hold together to a greater or lesser extent. It is *comprehensive* because it touches on everything we could believe, and it is a *framework* because it attempts to see how all this holds together.

Additionally, worldview involves our "basic beliefs about things." By 'basic,' Wolters means that worldview deals with the ultimate questions. "Who has pitched the most no-hitters in Major League history?" is not a question related to worldview, even if it is something we can say with confidence and conviction. Instead, worldview deals with big questions like "Who am I?," "What is the world?," "Where did everything come from?," "Where is everything headed?," "How do I make sense of change?," or even "Why is there evil in the world?" Worldview involves our basic beliefs, which show up in how we handle crisis, how we deal with disagreement, or simply how we navigate the world.

We all live as if certain answers to these questions are true. Even if we have never asked, "what is my life for?," we live an implicit answer to that question. Our lived answer may differ from what we would answer if asked, but none of us can avoid answering these large questions. Worldview is a way of thinking through these questions, seeking true answers, and seeing how everything holds together.

What began as a concept in Dutch and German theology now influences how many Reformed and Evangelical Christians pursue discipleship, apologetics, education, and even evangelism. Teaching students a Christian worldview and how to identify and respond to other (ultimately deficient) worldviews has become a staple of Christian schools and universities in North America.

BRAINS ON A STICK?

The concept of the "Christian worldview," however, has come under criticism in recent years. In particular, James K. A. Smith, who holds the Gary and Henrietta Byker Chair in Applied Reformed Theology and Worldview at Calvin College, has raised serious questions about how worldview is typically taught and whether it is an adequate tool for discipleship.

Smith argues that most teaching of Christian worldview includes an assumption about what it means to be human, what he calls "thinking-thingism" or "brains on a stick."[3] From Smith's perspective, the common teaching on worldview assumes that people are driven primarily by what they think. When worldview is taught primarily as an intellectual system, framework, or constellation of beliefs, we are implicitly claiming that what matters most about a person is what is going on in their mind. People are brains who happen to have a body. We can imagine this way of conceiving of a human person as having a huge and oversized brain but a small and inconsequential body ('brain on a stick'). While not confined to worldview, Smith would see this as connected with a belief that most problems of discipleship can be solved with more information. Education and discipleship are about getting the right ideas into people's heads and the wrong ideas out.

Smith believes this approach to discipleship and formation is misguided. Drawing from the insights of Augustine, he contends that, as humans, we are driven more by what we love than what we think[4] and he argues persuasively that secular consumer culture already understands this. The commercial for a new Lexus, for example, does not try to appeal to our brain, but to our desires. It is trying to sell us a lifestyle, not a car. Most advertising follows a similar strategy. If we buy this vehicle, we will be successful, sophisticated, and adored. If we buy this shampoo, women will love us. If we buy this software or masterclass, we will never worry about money again. If we wear these jeans, we will be the envy of other women. Most advertisements spend little time on the benefits of the product itself, because the goal is not to convince us logically or intellectually, but to get us to want what *they* (the popular, pretty, happy, successful, and loved people in the commercial) have, because we want to be like *them*. Advertisers want us to long for and crave products more than they want to convince us that we are making a logical choice.

This formation of desire is about worship, about where we direct our lives. It is ultimately, in Smith's view, religious. Smith gives extensive examples of how the mall and the stadium function as religious experiences. He looks at how architecture shapes our experiences and expectations. He explores the patterns of behavior (or 'liturgies') of both spaces.

- The opening ceremonies at a football stadium, with its imagery and singing of the national anthem, mold what we love and desire.
- At the mall, we are trained to manage anxiety through consumption. Each store becomes a little chapel, with acolytes who will guide us through the experience (customer service) and a priest (aka cashier) who will accept our offerings in exchange for peace and happiness in the form of an Old Navy polo shirt.

While it may initially seem odd to consider malls, commercials, and sporting events as religious experiences, we ignore them to our detriment. They shape what we love, which in turn, shapes how we live.

Smith asserts we are shaped not primarily by what we think, but by what we love. He is not arguing that thinking is unimportant, but only that thinking the right thoughts won't automatically lead us to virtue and faithfulness. We need love. We all know plenty of people who know all the right things, can check all the right doctrinal boxes, and yet show by their lives that what they really cherish is money, power, sex, prestige, security, or any of a number of lesser substitutes for God. Getting the right intellectual framework in place won't be enough to compel us to actually seek first the kingdom of heaven. Smith advocates a recovery of the centrality of worship and intentional practices (habits) as a means by which God shapes our loves so that we love the kingdom of Christ (and its King) and not the kingdoms of this world.

What does this have to do with Christian worldview? Smith's concern is that Christian discipleship often does not match how people are actually discipled. Churches and universities, particularly those focused on worldview, have — in Smith's estimation — centered on the brain and rational thought, forgetting the body and how practice shapes us as disciples. In Smith's words, "We could describe this as "bobble head" Christianity, so fixated on the cognitive that it assumes a picture of human beings that look like bobble heads: mammoth heads that dwarf an almost nonexistent body. In sum, because the church buys into a cognitivist anthropology, it adopts a stunted pedagogy that is fixated on the mind."[5] When we assume that what matters most is what we think, then our discipleship will seek only to get the right ideas into people's heads. This ignores a significant portion of how we are actually shaped in our daily lives. "From the pictures of Christians implied in worldview-talk, one would never guess that we become disciples by engaging in communal practices of baptism, communion, prayer, singing, and dancing."[6]

According to Smith, we need Christian worship more than we need a Christian worldview. "So if we want to discern the shape of a Christian worldview, it is crucial that we recall the priority of liturgy to doctrine. Doctrines, beliefs, and a Christian worldview emerge *from* the nexus of Christian worship practices; worship is the *matrix* of Christian faith, not its 'expression' or 'illustration.'"[7] Recovering the central place of worship and habit in discipleship will do more to shape our worldview than any number of books.

James K. A. Smith is correct that teaching worldview as an intellectual framework is insufficient. It is not enough to simply get all our thoughts ordered correctly in our heads. He is also right to point us to the formative practices of Christian worship as a way of growing deeper in love of Christ.[8] Humans are not primarily brains on a stick, but lovers, and we are moved more by our loves than by our thoughts. Smith's critique of worldview is accurate in that many modern forms of worldview fall into this form of rationalism and cognitivism. Christian discipleship and talk of worldview have often focused exclusively on ideas and neglected practice. We have sought to produce disciples by making certain they have the right worldview in their minds as well as have the intellectual tools to dismantle the false worldviews they will encounter. But by neglecting the formation of our hearts (and not just our minds), we run the distinct risk of producing disciples who acknowledge Jesus with their lips, but whose hearts are far from him.

Should we stop talking about worldview altogether? In this book, I will argue that the way forward is to go back. We should not abandon worldview, but, instead, call it back to its original purpose.

RECOVERING THE PURPOSE OF CHRISTIAN WORLDVIEW

Imagine a man sitting in a chair surrounded by balloons. As you watch, he takes a sewing needle, grabs a balloon, and pierces it. The balloon pops with a loud sound. He drops the remains of the first balloon and turns to pick up a second. The loud 'pop' signals that a second balloon has met its end. As he picks up a third, you walk over and ask him, "Why are you popping those balloons?" He gives you a puzzled look, "Isn't that what a needle is for?"

You pause. "Well, a needle *can* be used that way, but that is not really what it is for." You take his hand and lead him to a table at the back of the room. On the table is some blue thread and a pair of jeans with a rip in the knee. Threading the needle, you begin to stitch the tear in the jeans back together. As he watches, the look of puzzlement gives way to awe. Holding up the finished work, you say, "That is what a needle is for. It helps mend what has been torn."

Christian worldview is like a needle. Yes, it can be used to poke holes, but that is not what it is meant for. We should use it to mend what has been torn. The same is true with respect to worldview. Many have used worldview as a tool to poke holes in the thought-balloons — the worldviews, the philosophies, religions, or perspectives — of others. We know what we believe and we can easily find the faults, find the errors, or find the inconsistencies in the positions of others. We can then use the needle of worldview as an offensive or defensive weapon. With the consistency and logic of a Christian worldview, we can focus on defending the faith against falsehood and error. With its ability to analyze and dismantle other viewpoints, the Christian worldview can be used to defeat and potentially convert opponents to the truer and more coherent position — Christianity.

While it may be possible to use the Christian worldview as

a weapon, just as it may be possible to use a needle to poke holes in a balloon, to pretend that this is the primary purpose of the Christian worldview misses the point. Worldview is no more a weapon of destruction than is a needle. Instead, like the sewing needle, worldview is meant to mend.

Weaponizing worldview often runs afoul of many of the critiques that Smith lays out. It allows us to be intellectually prideful. It leads us to believe that having the right starting point is enough. It causes us to neglect the way we are shaped by forces outside of our intellect.

A proper understanding of worldview, however, one that mends rather than pierces, will stand alongside the insights given by Smith. An accurate understanding of worldview can take its place alongside worship as forming the whole person for life before the face of God. A recovery of Christian worldview can, in the words of Herman Bavinck, bring about "a wonderful unity subjectively between our thinking and doing, between our head and our heart."9

Worldview talk arose in a time of fracture, a time of sickness in the soul that feels pervasive in modern life. It came about at a time when the world seemed to be pulling itself apart at the seams. This fraying of life came about, as worldview proponents argued, because we had abandoned God. In Christ, all things hold together. Apart from him, things fall apart. The fractures in our understanding of knowledge, of the world around us, and of how we are to live in this world result from the removal of our center in Christ. The recovery of a theological center, of a robust faith in God that impacts all of life, serves as a way to sew back together what the modern world seeks to rip apart. Worldview gives voice to a way before and beyond the fractures, a world we have abandoned in order to rule ourselves. Like a needle, worldview is meant to mend.

A GUIDED TOUR BACK TO WORLDVIEW

In order to move forward in our thinking about worldview, we need to go back. However, we need not travel this path alone. We will use the work of the Dutch theologian Herman Bavinck as our guide. Born in 1854, Bavinck lived through the upheavals of the late modern world. He worked both as a theologian and professor of systematic theology to hold fast to the orthodox Christian (Reformed) faith while also addressing a constantly changing world. In 1904, he gave an address in Amsterdam that would become the first edition of *Christian Worldview*. He published a second, expanded edition in 1913. Though more than a hundred years separate Bavinck and us, the core challenges we face remain much the same. Though many of the trends Bavinck named have accelerated in our time, their substance is unchanged.

In *Christian Worldview*, Bavinck lays out the ways life has seemed to come apart in the modern world. With philosophical and theological precision, he details the modern shifts in three major areas:

- the relationship between thinking and being (knowledge)
- the relationship between being and becoming (the world)
- the relationship between becoming and action (morality)

In short, Bavinck saw his world falling into chaos, distress, and confusion because humans attempted to understand knowledge, the world, and morality apart from God. We had abandoned seeing God and everything in relationship to God. Apart from God, our worldview cannot hold together. In response, Bavinck explains how all things truly hold together in God. Bavinck sees worldview as a way of mending what has been torn in modernity and seeks to present just what that unified world looks like.

In *All Things Hold Together*, we will draw heavily from Bavinck's work while also translating it into more accessible language, all with an eye as to how this shows up in contemporary life. In Chapter 1, we will look at how life is fraying at the seams, exploring the various ways our world is accelerating and becoming more unstable. We will then explore the phenomenon of "Remixed Religion," where many modern people create their own curated religions to meet their felt needs. Into this context, we will set out the purpose of a Christian worldview, to sew back together all these scattered parts of our world and ourselves.

The remaining chapters work in pairs. Chapters 2 and 3 deal with the question of knowledge. In Chapter 2, we will look at the modern split between whether we know things primarily through thinking or through experience. Both are rooted in a desire to find an independent foundation for knowledge apart from God. However, as we will see, both substitute foundations ultimately crumble. We will conclude with the claim that it is only when we hold to God as Creator that we can truly know the world through both our experience and reflection.

In Chapter 3, we will dive deeper into how God the Creator makes it possible for us to have trustworthy knowledge of the world around us. The search for an independent foundation of knowledge led us to the fractured state in which we find ourselves. The way forward (and the way back) is to recover how all knowledge depends upon something, but that only God has the strength to hold together our knowledge of the world. Everything else eventually crumbles.

Chapters 4 and 5 will shift to wrestle with how we make sense of the world around us. In particular, how do we make sense of stability and change, as well as unity and diversity. If things are fundamentally stable and unchanging, then how can anything change at all? If everything always changes, can we trust anything? Is everything connected or unique?

In Chapter 4, we will see that the modern world separates into two main views. Either stability reigns supreme and we view the world like a great machine that has been wound up and set to go, or we view the world as a living, breathing thing, brimming with energy and flux. These ancient philosophical questions show up in the contemporary obsessions with efficiency, and the rising belief in "vibes" or "energy." However, neither of these positions can make sense of the presence and diversity of life. In response, the Christian worldview is organic — holding both unity and diversity together.

Chapter 5 explains in greater detail just what it means for the Christian worldview to be 'organic.' God is Triune, but his creation is organic — full of diversity and unity. Because of who God is and how he created the world, we can make sense of the stability of a changing world. There can be genuine development and change because God is leading history toward its fulfillment in the kingdom of God. But the world is also formed according to the unchanging wisdom of God.

Chapters 6 and 7 move toward considering the moral life. How shall we live in this world? Chapter 6 tells of two shifts that have precipitated the disintegration of our sense of the moral world. First, there is the shift from the family to the individual as the fundamental unit of morality. We see ourselves as isolated individuals and not as people who are embedded into covenantal relationships with one another. Second, the modern world has moved from recognizing an external moral law to humans making laws for themselves. "Humans as lawmakers" leads to either relativism or determinism — either alleging that all morality is relative to the time and culture, or simply denying morality altogether in favor of more therapeutic categories. Both undermine our ability to live well and wholly in this world. The solution is to recover God as the divine lawgiver.

Chapter 7 presents the case for God as the divine lawgiver by working through the three main beats of the biblical story — Creation, Fall, and Redemption. In creation, we see that God is the source of both physical and moral laws, creating a unified cosmos. In the Fall, we explore the various terms modernity has used to replace the category of sin and how they ultimately misdiagnose our problems. Lastly, we will recover a Christian account of history by exploring the history of God's work of redemption.

Throughout these chapters, we will work to keep in mind the concerns and insights of James K. A. Smith on discipleship and worldview. Mending what has been torn apart in modernity will take far more than getting the right ideas in place. It will take the grace of God working through ideas, practices, habits, communities, and institutions that will shape us to see the world as it truly is, even if for the first time.

CHAPTER 1
MADE TO MEND
WORLDVIEW IN A FRAYED WORLD

> *"What strikes us in the modern age is the internal discord that consumes the self and the restless haste that drives it."*
> - Herman Bavinck

> *"The mass of men lead lives of quiet desperation."*
> - Henry David Thoreau

It's Sunday afternoon and you are playing in the backyard. Your parents told you to take off your dress pants, but you promised you'd be careful. You're halfway up a tree when you slip, or you're chasing someone in a game of tag and you trip. The next thing you know, you are on the ground, your knee bloody, and there's a hole in your new pants.

Your mom swiftly washes and bandages your knee. She runs the pants through the wash, removing the dirt and blood, but the rip remains. Then she sits down with the pants across her lap, pulls out a needle and thread, and begins to sew them back together.

Christian worldview is like that — it's the thread that sews back together the rips that have been opened by the modern world. The ever-increasing demands of modern life, coupled with accelerating technological and social change, leave many of us frayed and fractured. At the same time, more and more people are abandoning traditional orthodox Christianity in favor of a more personally-crafted and fluid spirituality. In a world being pulled apart, these remixed religions or sophisticated philosophies cannot help us grapple with the world as it is. Only Christianity can mend what has been torn.

Before we identify the details of a Christian worldview, we need to take stock of our current moment and of the vacuum created by the lack of a coherent Christian worldview. We will look first at how the absence of a unifying center causes our culture to swing to extremes, leading to improvement in some areas of our lives and increased misery in others. Then we will examine the impact of the breakdown of religious identity and the blurring of religious practice in the West. Third, we will look at Christian worldview as a means of receiving the world as it truly is, dealing with reality as a whole, rather than only addressing some of its parts. Lastly, we will explore what it means for this worldview to be unifying, a way of mending the fissures brought on by the modern world.

LIFE FRAYING AT THE SEAMS

You hold on for dear life as the merry-go-round spins faster and faster. As a young child, you feel the thrill of it trying to fling you off. Your best friend, your big brother, or your dad runs along the outside, pushing hard and making you go even faster. You tighten your grip and beg them to stop. Thankfully, they eventually stop pushing. The merry-go-round slows down, comes to a stop, and you stumble off dizzily.

What might excite us as a young child can be nauseating when we become adults. The greater the speed on the merry-go-round, the more force trying to fling us off. As adults, most of us choose not to ride anymore. We no longer desire the disorientation and chaos.

That's the challenge of contemporary life — most of us feel like we are stuck on a merry-go-round, going ever faster and faster. The pace of life only seems to be accelerating, changing more and more, leaving us feeling more and more fragmented. Technology that seemed cutting edge a couple years ago is now woefully outdated. Social changes seem to come rapidly too, often too fast for us to fully comprehend, let alone evaluate and engage. What would have been unthinkable fifty years ago, and improbable just twenty years ago, is commonplace today.

Even the pace of daily life seems only to be increasing. Adult life feels, for many of us, like an incessant race against time, debt, and inflation (which we run with a job and a couple side hustles). It feels like a never-ending struggle to try and have the life we were promised we could have, if only we were willing to put in a little hard work. The more we work, though, the more we sense that, if we stop for more than a few minutes, we will be swept under and drown.

Even as we celebrate some of the changes in contemporary life (and lament others), we often discover that it is the pace of change that feels so overwhelming. Our life feels like that merry-go-round spinning faster and faster. The more quickly things change the more we fear that we will be thrown off completely, sent bruised and tumbling to the ground.

For some of us, the feeling may be similar to a piece of fabric being pulled at every corner. As the tension from every side increases, the fabric starts to tear. We fear that if these tears are not repaired soon, the whole cloth may be torn to pieces. We — our society, our world — feels more and more like that piece of cloth.

We are not the first to feel this way.

Over a century ago, the Dutch theologian Herman Bavinck described the turn of the 20th century as "rapidly advancing."

He saw it as a time of significant and rapid change, when people sought to understand what defined the times, and what would provide direction for the future. Some pointed to political changes, saying this was the era of freedom and democracy (or anarchy and totalitarianism). Others focused on economic or scientific developments, such as the rise of capitalism or the application of the scientific method to all areas of life. Still others turned to the new ways of viewing human life and ethics: psychology, relativism, increased personal choice.[1]

Bavinck believed there might be some element of truth in many or most of these options, but argued that they all missed the fullness of what it meant to live as a modern person. "What strikes us in the modern age is the internal discord that consumes the self and the restless haste that drives it."[2] Bavinck saw a disharmony, a disunity, a fraying and fracture at the heart of modern life.

We have seen incredible advances in science and technology, since Bavinck first examined the state of the world more than a hundred years ago. Advances in medications, vaccination, surgical procedures, physical therapy, and a variety of treatments have turned once fatal or disabling conditions into minor inconveniences. What we now understand about biology, chemistry, and physics has opened up incredible possibilities for genuine good for human life on earth.

However, even when there are advancements in one area of life, there will often be increased misery in others. As Alan Noble insightfully notes in his book, *You Are Not Your Own*, "Another way that society fails to fulfill its promise is by introducing new problems to solve old ones as society progresses."[3] The promise of modern progress (whether in medicine, science, economics, politics, or social mores) is that it will improve life. However, even as modern life solves one problem, it often creates others. You might take a pill to treat your high blood pressure. However, that pill has the side effect of gastric reflux, so you need a second pill to treat the symptoms created by the first. However, that second pill has its own side effects. Eventually either we resign ourselves to an ever-increasing cocktail of pills to treat our increasing list of symptoms, or we learn to live with problems we never would have had otherwise.

What is true in medicine is true of much of modern life. Political and economic solutions to one problem end up creating others. Social changes may improve one area of life (or life for one set of people) but increase misery in another. Modern prescriptions for life always come with a list of side effects.

We see so much "improvement" in the world, but also feel a deep discontent or despair. Alan Noble sums up contemporary life by saying, "...while there are moments of joy, nobody seems to be actually flourishing — except on Instagram, which only makes us feel worse."[4] It is not only our world that seems to be falling apart, but we, as human beings, can feel like we are fraying at the seams.

Bavinck sees the root of the problems in the modern world as 'internal discord.' We have all this knowledge, all these intellectual disciplines, all this technique and love and feelings and longings, but we have nothing that holds it all together. Instead of a beautiful mosaic, we have a loose pile of colored tiles that form nothing. Each tile would be good in its place, would contribute to the beauty of the mosaic, but cut off from the others, it sees itself as the only tile that matters.

Centuries before Bavinck, Augustine said that peoples and nations were bound together by "a common agreement as to the objects of their love."[5] Part of the crisis of our current world is that we lack a common agreement on what we love and are, therefore, deeply divided and fractured as a people. In Augustine's definition, we have ceased to be a people at all. Without the love of God at the center, we are each left with lesser, earthly loves and we seek to put together the pieces of life on our own.

Lacking a coherent vision of what the world truly is, who we are, and how we are to live in it (basically, without a worldview), our modern world pushes toward extremes. We see a divide between radical individualism and fanatical dedication to community, between realism and symbolism in art and literature, between "narrow-minded chauvinism" and "humanity without fatherland," between nature and nurture in development. Our western culture swings back and forth between these various extremes, struggling to land because we cannot hold all the truth together without also holding on to God.[6]

Our inability to understand and see how all things are held together leads us to seek to form our own images from the various mosaic tiles or, more often, to try to form the world in our own image. This fracturing in the modern world impacts every area of life, including religious belief.

REMIXED RELIGION

He's a Christian minister, but regularly promotes Buddhist meditation. She studies her Bible, but also consults a horoscope and believes in reincarnation. After drinking his carefully crafted smoothie to help cleanse his body of toxins, he goes to Mass, then spends the afternoon reading and contemplating the works of the Stoics. Whether these shared convictions can be made to make sense together is beside the point for many people. An eclectic spirituality that best serves our personal quest for meaning has quickly become the norm.

Our contemporary world has seemed to move beyond orthodox Christianity. Identification with a particular religion is declining in America (and across the West). More people check "none" when asked their religious affiliation (a group often called the Nones) and more people identify as "spiritual but not religious" (SBNRs). Interestingly, outright atheism is not on the rise, but people are less likely to claim one religion than in generations before. Instead, people say they are "spiritual," drawing from different sources and finding their own way to make sense of the world without "organized religion."

In her book, *Strange Rites: New Religions for the Godless World*, Tara Isabella Burton describes this phenomenon as "Remixed Religion." Americans are not abandoning faith altogether, but cobbling together a personal playlist of what they believe best suits their needs and desires and helps them make sense of the world. A little Buddhist meditation here, a dash of the Serenity Prayer here, consult a psychic when you need one.

Syncretism, or the blending of religious traditions, is nothing new. Sometimes this blending happens unconsciously and other times after periods of intentional reflection and even personal struggle. However, with the advent of the internet and a decline in broader trust in institutions, we see religious blending or 'remixing' taking place on an increasingly personal level. As Burton states, "What we are seeing now isn't just an increase in culturally specific syncretism, but religious fluidity on a personal level."[7] We also observe this in our "increasing willingness to blur the boundaries of religious traditions, and to pick and choose what suits us."[8]

In short, more people make their own religion now. We borrow what works for us, what meets our needs, or what helps us cope or get where we want to go. However, this phenomenon of 'remixing' is not something that only affects those who don't claim a specific religion. It is in the church as well.

Think of New Age beliefs, for example. While not exactly a dogmatic religion, it might include things such as astrology, reincarnation, psychics, and the location of spiritual energy within physical objects. These beliefs are incredibly common in the wider culture, but also, perhaps surprisingly, within the church. Burton notes: "About 60 percent of the religiously unaffiliated believed in at least one of these phenomena. But what is most striking about the poll is that *so did an almost identical percentage of Christians...*In other words, the personal beliefs and practices of self-identifying Christians are themselves increasingly varied."[9] The boundary lines have become blurred to the point that "[a]t least half of America — and likely far more — is either a faithful None, an SBNR, or a religiously flexible hybrid."[10]

Remixing religion entails a certain kind of rejection of orthodox institutional Christianity. A personally curated religious experience is not synonymous with "the faith once for all delivered to the saints" (Jude 3). While all Christian faith is deeply personal in one sense, it is not personalized. Christianity is only ever *about us* in a secondary sense. It is first and foremost about God and who he is and what he has done. As the Westminster Catechism says, the chief end (goal, purpose) of man is to "glorify God and enjoy him forever." We are brought into God's story, adopted through God's gracious action, but it is not our story first.

However, personalization is precisely the point of remixing faith. Not every aspect of any given religion is seen to meet our felt needs. To flourish as humans, we need to find what works for us (or so we think). The goal of remixing is personalization, not exactly coherence. It doesn't matter as much whether these religious beliefs and practices can be put together into a sensible whole. What matters is whether it is meaningful *for me*, whether it helps *me* feel closer to God/the divine, whether it fits with *my* social and political sensibilities, or helps *me* get through the day with a little peace.

We want our religion hand-crafted, just like the specialty messenger bag we bought at that boutique. We want it designed for us, like the companies that ask us to fill out a survey and they will send us just the right coffee beans for our taste, just the perfect sweater for us, or just what we wanted (even if we didn't know it before they charged our credit card).

This remixing of religion occurs side-by-side with the fracture of modern life. The strain caused by the increased pace of life and ever-increasing options, as well as the "inherent discord" of modern life, leaves the fabric of faith feeling as if it is in tatters. And it's not just Christianity — every religion and every belief system feels frayed. As we oscillate between our various options and as the pace of life threatens to tear us apart or hurl us into the distance, we grope for a way to put together the pieces of our lives.

Without anything inherently to hold our life and the world together, we are each left to make sense of it on our own. We strive to make the best and most fulfilling picture we can with the mosaic tiles still in our grasp.

What if these two phenomena are related? What if the fracture in modern life is caused by the rejection of Christian faith?

I believe that the rise of personalized, 'remixed' faith is connected to the fraying and fracturing of our worldview. Technology might make it easier and more comfortable to curate a religion than ever before, but the desire to do so arises from the sense that something is broken in the modern world, and from our belief that the options we have been given to make sense of the world seem to fail. We seek to create our own "cafeteria-style" religion because we have been told that the only path forward is to make a way for ourselves.

In reflecting on the challenges of modern life, Bavinck saw an intimate connection between a rejection of Christian faith and the fracture we experience as modern people. He saw the rise of extremism (political, philosophical, and social) as rooted in a rejection of the Christian faith.

Imagine two forces pulling on opposite ends of a rope — if the rope snaps, they will careen in opposite directions. While the rope holds, though, the opposing sides cannot move as far as they would like to go.

Bavinck sees the roots of modern civilization as a rejection of Christianity, an attempt to sever the rope that holds all things together. This is why, he believes, our culture has seen such a dramatic rise in extremism — there is nothing holding it together. "Between socialism and individualism, between democracy and aristocracy, between classicism and Romanticism, between atheism and pantheism, between unbelief and superstition, civilized humanity swings back and forth."[11]

For all their differences, the extremists of our modern world seem to agree on one thing: Christianity had its day and is fading fast. It no longer fits with 'what we know now.' Our modern world seeks to build knowledge, the world, and morality on a new non-theological (and therefore, atheistic) foundation.

In the coming chapters, we will join Bavinck in exploring the various fracture points in modern life, looking at how the Christian faith points to the one who can truly hold all things together. For now, it is important enough that we see the connection between the fragmentation of life and the rise of remixed religions. Both have their root in an abandonment of the God who reveals himself in Scripture.

In Bavinck's time, as our own, people explored exotic places and exotic philosophies, borrowing from many sources (including the occult), and making everything an object of divinity. "While it is not only [seen like] this, religion has become, for many, a private matter, which they arrange to their own liking."[12] Quite often, these 'new religions' often seek to be 'this worldly' to repair, to fix, or to contrast with the 'otherworldly' Christian faith.

Bavinck claims the rejection of Christianity is the cause of the fracture we experience in our souls and the soul of our culture. Here Bavinck anticipates Burton by more than a hundred years, "It is precisely the loss of religion that gives rise to the inventors of new religions everywhere — and in great numbers."[13] The rejection of Christianity and the Christian worldview is not necessarily the rejection of faith altogether or the rejection of spirituality and religious experience. When the modern world rejects the Christian faith, that void will still seek to be filled, this time by the plethora of personal pieties and practices we choose as part of our life journey.

Bavinck is strikingly cheerful about the prospects for the Christian faith. While he says that, "Christianity stands antithetically to all that is brought before the market today under the name *religion*," he also says that "The Christian religion views this seeking and groping of a corrupt humanity not with indifference but rather with a sublime peace and even a joyful certainty."[14] Far from being discouraged or disheartened by the questing and religious remixing of our contemporary world, Bavinck argues that we should have 'joyful certainty.' If we are looking to make sense of the world, make sense of ourselves, or even make sense of what we should do with our lives, there is ultimately only one place we can go that can truly satisfy: God. Even as Christianity stands against all the rival and substitute religions (by whatever name they are called), we do so not with fearful defensiveness, but with confidence that if we truly want to face the world as it is, only Christianity will enable us to do that.

WELCOME TO THE REAL WORLD

For Bavinck, the solution is not a return to some golden age, nor is it to try and undo modernity. Instead, we need to learn to embrace the world as it truly is. It is not enough to have a cohesive set of beliefs, convictions, or practices, ones that fit neatly together. Our beliefs, convictions, and practices must also correspond with reality.

Contemporary remixed religions fall short on both accounts. It is impossible to hold astral charts, witchcraft, and Tibetan prayer beads together in a coherent way. Even if we could, it doesn't match how the world actually works. However, it is not just pop religion and spiritual gurus on Instagram and Oprah who have this problem. As we will explore in the coming chapters, even sophisticated and supposedly 'scientific' systems fail to fully account for the world as it is.

One of the strengths of the Christian worldview — and the reason we can view all the religious searching with confidence — is that the world and everything in it was made by God. To believe in God and to confess how that belief shapes everything else in the world is not to superimpose an ideology on the world. The world is not a flat, dull nature with a religious overlay, as is so often argued by proponents of modernity. Instead, the world is a creation of the Creator. This is how the world truly is.

If we look only at whether a worldview or system of thought makes internal sense, we might be able to say there are many different worldviews (though Bavinck would doubt this). But when it comes to claims making sense with one another and matching the real world as it actually is, there is only one true 'world and life view.' Only Christianity takes things as they really are. It is the only religion whose view of the world truly fits the world.

> "Whoever shakes off the idols of the day and knows to rise above the prevailing prejudices in science and the academy, who faces up to the things themselves, soberly and watchfully, and takes the world and humanity, nature and religion as they truly are in themselves, presses on, evermore strengthening the conviction that Christianity is the only religion whose view of the world and life fits the world and life."[15]

Our contemporary life feels so chaotic and miserable, in part because we have structured our lives and societies in ways that do not match the real world. Instead of receiving the world as it is, we seek to remake it as we see fit. We operate on a false understanding of knowledge, of the world, and of morality and our ship ultimately runs aground when it strikes reality.

It's like the story of three blind men who each come in contact with a different part of an elephant. One touches the elephant's side and becomes convinced that the whole elephant is like a rock, solid and strong. The second one feels the elephant's trunk, noting how it moves and twists like a snake — he pictures an animal whose whole body is like that of a snake. The last man grabs the leg of the elephant and envisions a creature built like a tree. Each man is correct about what he touches, but each speaks falsely when claiming that the part he touched represents the whole elephant.

Similarly, it's not that different disciplines and positions of our modern world don't speak some level of truth. Like the blind men with the elephant, the many different disciplines — science, politics, economics, philosophy, psychology, among others — are all often quite good at identifying what they specifically touch. However, in rejecting God, our modern world has left us blind to the elephant. Each discipline believes that what it knows to be true in its small arena of study must, therefore, be true for the whole of reality. While these disciplines all may speak some truth, none of them taken individually consider or understand the whole. Only with our eyes opened in faith in God can we see the elephant, see how the tree trunk legs, the snake-like trunk, and the rock-like sides are held together by the reality of the elephant.

It is the contention of this book that we cannot truly make sense of the world, ourselves, and what we are to do with our lives apart from faith in God. A Christian worldview is the articulation of what it means to take reality as it truly is — a creation of the God who has revealed himself in Holy Scripture. A common claim in our contemporary culture contends that Christianity cannot stand up to the intellectual and social challenges of the contemporary world, that it will soon be consigned to the dustbin of history. At the very least, it must be updated to address modern problems unanticipated by ancient Christians. Such a claim not only reveals a profound ignorance of the intellectual and moral challenges faced by Christians throughout the ages, but also a profound belief in the inadequacy of the Christian faith. The constant updating and remixing within and outside of the church reveals a deep insecurity about Christianity's ability to face the challenges of the present age.

I will argue in this book that only Christianity can help us effectively respond to the challenges of the present age (or any age). Far from being flat-footed or thrown off-kilter by the storms of the present, the Christian faith is uniquely equipped to help us navigate the present moment. Why? Because it is *true*. As true, the Christian worldview matches the world as it truly is. This means we can be humble before the Lord but also confident in Christianity's ability to address the big questions.

God holds together the fabric of reality. Even though there may be discoveries or questions that surprise us, they do not surprise God. We do not make the world, but we take it as it is, which requires acknowledging who made it and who rules it. "The idea of Christianity and the meaning of reality belong together like lock and key: they make sense together."[16]

MENDING THE TEARS

In the coming chapters, we will follow Bavinck in looking at three of the major fracture points in our modern culture: How can and do we know anything? How do we make sense of change? How are we supposed to live? With each question, we will begin with the fractures. We will look at the prevailing contemporary options and demonstrate how they cannot hold together and how they do not match reality. Then we will turn to see how Christian faith more adequately addresses these deep questions and mends the tears created by the modern world.

However, there are two more things we need to understand about a Christian worldview before we move forward in more detail. First, the unifying nature of the Christian faith is not about mediating or finding compromise between competing claims. That gets the situation backwards. While initially we will be talking about the fractures, because that is how we experience the world right now, we must remember that unity comes first. The world *is* as God has made it — that is what a Christian worldview tries to articulate. The fractures and fraying we experience are a departure from that truth, from that original unity.

The difference is important. Imagine that a Christian worldview was simply about finding the happy medium between the claims of the world. That would be like taking two separate and distinct pieces of cloth and sewing them together into one new thing. They might not necessarily belong together, but something can be made of them, depending on what they looked like when you started. If the Christian worldview was about making unity out of division, it would assume the world did not belong together as a whole. It would also have to start with what the world says in order to form what the church says.

Instead, Christianity opposes all idols of the day by treating reality as it is. Christianity does not 'fit' the deviant concepts of the modern world — it opposes them. There is a cloth — reality as it truly is — and it has begun to fray and it has tears in it. The Christian worldview, by speaking of the whole cloth, who made it, and what it was made for, begins to sew back together some of the places that have ripped. It restores our knowledge, our sense of the world, and our morality back to its prior unity in faith in God. Christian worldview is more like mending a torn garment than making a new one from several unmatched pieces.

While Bavinck does believe that Christianity holds together what the world has ripped apart, it is not a mediating position or a reconciliation of opposites. In part, this is because Christianity is the default, not the division.[17] The division is created by the rejection of Christian faith. Thus, the Christian faith does not have to mediate between two existing opposites. Instead, it can simply positively hold out its claims, which will be a unified world-and-life view, because it is true, not because we managed to manufacture some compromise. Though we will address the fractures first, we must always remember that it is for the sake of repairing and restoring a forgotten unity, not for forging a new one.

Second, simply adopting a Christian worldview is not going to fix all our problems. The challenge and fractures of the modern world are not only a matter of belief or unbelief, but of design. We have designed our world, with its social structures, technologies, and institutions. As Alan Noble notes, these designs are not neutral. "The designers (who happen to be us, by the way: only humans are capable of creating inhuman environments for themselves) had a particular idea of the human person in mind when they created the modern world."[18] So even if everyone in our town, state, or country suddenly converted to Christianity tomorrow and started to hold a Christian worldview, we would still live in a world structured and directed for life apart from God. We would still live in a fallen world full of fallen institutions — even the church participates in this fallenness. Noble accurately states that "Christians in America are carriers of contemporary disease too. Like the rest of Western society, the church in the West tends to be good at helping people cope with modern life, but not at undoing the disorder of modern life."[19] As good as learning and living a Christian worldview is in the world, it is not a path to comfort and ease. Instead, it is an invitation to struggle in an inhuman world.

Though a Christian worldview is about proclaiming the unity and diversity of the world as it is made by God, it is not an immediate pathway to peace. As Bavinck says, "The times are too grave to flirt with the spirit of the age. The deep, sharp contrast standing between the Christian faith and the modern person must provide us with the insights that picking portions of each is not possible and that deciding between alternatives is a duty. However lovely peace would be, the conflict is upon us."[20] We do not need to be afraid, though. In Christ, all things truly do hold together.

CONCLUSION

Life in the modern world seems to be fraying at the seams. As Alan Noble says, "Standards are never settled. Everything is always in flux."[21] It is a time of change and instability. While some change may be an improvement, there are also myriad ways that life is growing more inhumane. Alongside these intellectual and societal shifts is a religious one. More people are moving away from traditional religious identity to form a "remixed" faith on their own terms.

Drawing from the work of Herman Bavinck, we see that these two phenomena are linked. At the heart of the modern world is an internal discord caused by a rejection of the Christian faith. This discord leads contemporary life to swing back and forth between extremes and causes modern people to believe they must forge an identity, a purpose, and a sense of meaning for themselves.

Into this situation, there is a need to articulate a Christian worldview, not as a means of defeating opponents, but as a way to mend the cracks opened by modernity. The Christian faith has the resources to address the big questions of the contemporary world because it seeks to comprehend the world as it really is, not as we would like it to be. It is a world created and sustained by God.

Though this book will largely deal with the intellectual questions facing us in the modern world, a Christian worldview is not simply an intellectual project. It is not a matter of merely getting the right information in our heads or rearranging our mental furniture. At its core, Christian worldview is a way of engaging with the three chief theological virtues: faith, hope, and love. Christian worldview is recovering faith and trust in God as the center of human life in the world. It is recovering hope by recalling all things to their proper end and seeing all things in light of their destiny. A Christian worldview is profoundly hopeful because the world belongs to God. Christian worldview is also driven and animated by the love of God.

These virtues, as well as the intellectual and theological framework we will detail in this book, are grown and nurtured not primarily in the classroom or study, but in the home and sanctuary. One of the best ways we can begin to be shaped into the Christian worldview is to gather with God's people in worship. It is not just ripped pants that can be mended around the table at home, but many of the fractures of modern life. By being shaped to place our faith, hope, and love in God, we are already most of the way there to a Christian worldview. All that remains is to work this out in the various spheres of life and learning.

CHAPTER 2
FLYING HALF A SHIP
KNOWLEDGE IN THE MODERN WORLD

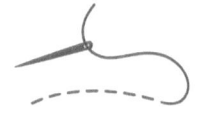

"All knowledge consists in the conformity of our consciousness to the objective truth. One thus knows the truth to the extent that he himself is in the truth. To understand the truth, one must be of the truth."
- Herman Bavinck

"Not to worry. We're still flying half a ship."
- Obi-Wan Kenobi

During a daring rescue mission, Obi-Wan Kenobi and Anakin Skywalker fight through droids and the Separatist leaders in order to rescue the Supreme Chancellor of the Republic. Having defeated or chased off the kidnappers, they commandeer the ship and head for safety. Anakin sits in the cockpit and seeks to pilot the damaged ship. The result is more a controlled crash than anything that could be called 'flying.' At one point, the cockpit lurches and the camera cuts to show that the entire back half of the ship has broken off and plummeted to the ground. Anakin remarks to Obi-Wan, "We lost something." Obi-Wan's quick reply: "Not to worry. We're still flying half a ship."[1]

Trying to talk about how we know things in the contemporary world feels like flying half a ship. On the one hand, our culture valorizes personal experience. If we have not lived it, we do not know it. On the other hand, our culture lifts up the mind and the intellect over and against our frail, mortal, and often frustrating bodies. Mind over matter. Brain over body. Choosing either option feels like we need to leave a significant part of human life and human knowledge behind. Like Obi-Wan, we might put on a cheerful face, but flying half a ship is nothing more than a controlled crash.

In what follows, we will look at the two halves of the ship of knowledge in our contemporary world — thought and experience, mind and body. We will look at the problems with each as well as where and how they show up in our contemporary life. We will then reflect on how we generally don't pick just one half of the broken ship, but try to fly both halves at once, even when the ship is broken. We will draw from the works of Alan Noble, James K. A. Smith, and Charles Taylor to understand how our secular age puts particular pressure on us to hold often contradictory beliefs and to hold all our beliefs with less conviction, less confidence, and less certainty. Lastly, we will begin to detail how a Christian worldview presents a unified ship of knowledge, allowing us to receive trustworthy knowledge from both our experience in the world and our reflection upon the world.

However, we must recognize something before we go any further. We don't begin life doubting or questioning whether we can truly know and understand the world. We assume that there is a world outside of us and that we can know it. We begin with a faith and a confidence that we can truly know things. We don't ask *how* we know until we are already *in the middle* of knowing things. Questions arise only when we pause and reflect on *how* we can actually know the world. Faith in our ability to know is the starting point of all knowledge. Doubt only enters later.

THE HALF-SHIP OF EXPERIENCE

What grounds this confidence, this faith we have that there is an outside world and that we can know it? For much of the history of philosophy, but particularly in the modern period, there have been two generally accepted answers to this question: empiricism and rationalism. We can trust experience (empiricism) or reason (rationalism). In the words of Bavinck, "For as long as the human being has occupied himself with this problem, he almost always ends up on one side or another, either sacrificing knowledge to being or being to knowledge."[2] Bavinck's language of 'knowledge' and 'being' is a way of talking about how we relate the things that exist in the world to the thinking that goes on in our minds. When it comes to knowledge, we tend to trust either our five senses or our ability to think. When we choose one approach, we end up sacrificing or minimizing the other.

According to the empiricists, we can only know what we can see, hear, taste, touch, or smell. These are our only trustworthy sources of knowledge. When we move away from the information we gather from our senses, we move away from reality into abstraction. We might need ideas or intellectual concepts to help us interpret what we take in from our senses, but those concepts are not ultimately real. They are nothing more than a handy mental device we use to group these sensations together.

Let's consider what an empiricist believes I can actually know when my cat crawls onto my lap. Light reflects off of an object in such a way that it enters my eyes and stimulates the rods and cones there. My brain interprets those sensations as colors (black and white) in the shape of a cat. Rhythmic vibrations in the air enter my ear. My brain translates these vibrations as a familiar sound (purring). I feel the weight and warmth of something pressing on my legs and a softness as I run my hand over the object in my lap. When I put all these sensations together and interpret them through the filter of other times that I have experienced a similar set of sensations, I deduce that what has happened is that the cat has walked across the couch, sat on my lap, and is now purring.

However, for the strict empiricist, 'cat' is merely a shorthand for a specific set of sensations. I do not genuinely know the 'cat,' but only the sensations I interpret to be a cat. I step away from the sensations, step away from what I see, hear, touch, taste, and smell, and group them together in a way that I can understand and call that concept 'cat.' It's not that the empiricist does not believe there is a cat on my lap — only that I cannot know that directly.

To the empiricist, the cat may or may not be real, but the concept of 'cat' is not a real thing. Instead, it is "nothing but "the breath of a voice," bearing no sounds, only merely a "concept of the mind."[3] Ideas are words we use to group experiences so we can understand them. An idea or concept itself is not real, but only a mental scaffold to help us interpret the world. We cannot know the things of this world directly, only the experiences we have of them. "Representations and concepts do not thus correspond to an objective reality but are abbreviations, "thought symbols" for a group of elements that usually appear in connection with each other."[4] Concepts, whether of physical things like cats, dogs, and boats or of deeper things like justice, truth, and beauty, have only a psychological value to us, as temporary aids to orient us in the world.

If this sounds a little extreme, it is. Yet, consider the way our culture views experience. For many, experience is the ultimate source of knowledge. Without personally experiencing something, we cannot truly "know" it.

Of course, experience is a very effective teacher. As Mark Twain said, "A man who carries a cat by the tail learns a lesson he can learn in no other way."[5] There are some things that are learned in particular ways through personal experience. No amount of music theory will offer the same kind of knowledge as seeing U2 live in concert at Soldier Field in Chicago. Reading a cookbook is a very different experience than making a recipe and eating the food.

However, there is a difference between personal experience as an effective learning tool and personal experience as the only way to learn something. The challenge of empiricism (and ultimately its error) is not that it says we can learn things from experience or that our sensations are a reliable source of knowledge. Instead, it is that it views these as the *only* reliable source of knowledge. It errs when it insists that concepts are merely abstractions and not real, that they are mildly useful at best and more often than not dangerous.

The basic tenets of empiricism, with its emphasis on the priority of experience, have now been applied to humanity and human nature. There is a powerful belief in our culture that "no one else can know what it is like to be me," because no one else has had the same set of experiences we each individually have. All I am — all that is *me* — is the set of experiences that I have. We define our 'self' as simply the way that we each individually group our experiences together. Ultimately that leads to the conclusion that our 'self' is not real in any objective sense, but only the sum total of our experiences.

It might seem like an odd philosophical curiosity to say that 'cat' is a concept used to describe a grouping of sensations or experiences, but what happens when we say the same of 'self' or 'humanity'? The belief, in many contemporary circles, is that we cannot truly know or understand someone whose experience is different than our own. Regardless of the distinguishing factor, whether it be race, sex, sexual identity, nationality, or even exposure to trauma, there is a conviction that if we have not lived it, we cannot know it. Taken to its logical extreme, the belief that personal experience is the only true source of knowledge necessarily leads us to conclude that we can never truly know another human being, nor any object in the world.

Tara Isabella Burton sees a similar phenomenon occurring in social justice circles. Though she doesn't use the language of empiricism and doesn't write strictly about how we come to know things, Burton sees a certain priority of experience — located in the body — as fundamental to the social justice movement. "Embodiment — and the subjective vision of truth it represents — is integral to social justice culture more broadly. Social justice culture valorizes not only the body as the site of meaning, but also what is termed lived experience: the specific and embodied knowledge that one can attain only by existing within one's various identities. Different forms of oppression... lead to human experiences so distinct from one another that they're barely translatable from one group of people to another."[6] Though Burton doesn't use these words, there is, in this form of empiricism, a rejection of any fundamental human nature. Our experience is so distinct that it is difficult — perhaps nearly impossible — to say that we all belong to the same group called 'humanity.'

Few use this language explicitly in our contemporary culture. However, when experience is touted as the only source of knowledge, concepts and ideas become suspect. These abstractions, these attempts to step away from experience itself and from our specific stories, do violence to our stories (and even to our selves). Burton says, "Our perceptions — our thoughts, our feelings, our responses, our lived experiences — are inherently authoritative. Likewise, assaults upon our perceptions have the same ontological status as physical violence. Microaggressions and misgendering aren't just immoral per se, but an assault upon the embodied self."[7] In short, every concept can be questioned, but no one would dare question our experience.

Let's step back from the social justice movement to consider it as one contemporary instance of empiricism and as an example of how empiricism, as a theory of knowledge, has real world consequences. Empiricism is not just about "can we know things through experience and our senses?" but "is experience the only way we come to know something?" When that second road is taken, it ultimately leads to the breakdown of knowledge. Why? Because while we can know our sensations, we cannot know what our sensations point to. While we can know our experience, we cannot know the experience of others. It follows, then, that we cannot truly know one another unless we share a significant overlap in personal experience. Even then, it may be difficult or impossible.

In Bavinck's terms, empiricism breaks the harmony between the subject and the object. It creates a fracture between "the knower" and the thing we are trying to know. That leaves us with mere perception, but without knowledge of the reality itself. I can know your actions and how I perceive them, but I cannot know you.

We see a contemporary manifestation of this impulse in our culture's views of personal experience. According to our culture, my truth, my story, my identity and everything I know comes from my personal experience — and so does yours. Whatever we share in common can only come from shared experience.

THE HALF SHIP OF THOUGHT

If empiricism centers on experience and contains a profound mistrust of concepts and ideas, rationalism is its opposite. The world and all its sense perceptions are unstable and changing. They do not offer us true knowledge of the essence of things. Real knowledge comes only from our mind. We only learn the truth through self-reflection.

The categories of trust and mistrust are important here. While empiricism and rationalism are theories about how we come to know things, they are, at heart, about trust. They are attempts to find a justification for how we can trust what we know. Empiricism finds all mental representations and ideas to be untrustworthy as a basis for knowledge because they are, in its view, detached from reality. By contrast, rationalism profoundly mistrusts our sense perceptions. How good are our eyes, really? How sensitive is our hearing? Even with expertly tuned instruments, there are variations and errors. Can we really trust what our senses tell us?

The point of rationalism is not whether we experience sight, sound, or touch, but whether we can trust that our senses will actually get us to the truth. The rationalists would argue that they do not.

René Descartes is universally considered the father of this form of skepticism. In an attempt to establish what he believed to be a rock solid and unshakeable foundation for knowledge, Descartes took a skeptical approach. Instead of trying to identify everything he knew to be true, he systematically identified everything that he believed could be doubted. He explored whether he really knew that there was a wax candle on his table. He questioned whether he really knew that he was sitting in his room. He doubted the entire existence of the outside world. He even doubted the existence of God. All he found left, when he finished, was his self and his mind.

This process ultimately led to Descartes' famous conclusion: "I think therefore I am." Descartes argued that, even if he knew nothing else, he knew that he was thinking about things. If he was thinking about those things, there had to be a René

Descartes doing the thinking. Once he set the foundation of his self and his own thinking mind, Descartes set out to 'prove' the existence of everything else: God, the world, his body, the wax candle on his table.[8] As Descartes worked to rebuild a comprehensive system of knowledge of the world, he used the foundation of his own mind, of his own thinking. He then concluded that, though the rest of the world may exist, it is only our minds and our thoughts that can be trusted.

If this, too, seems a little extreme, it is.[9] However, consider how our society views the function, process, and goals of education and learning. For large swaths of our culture, the point of education is to get the right information into our heads. There is a strong belief that as soon as we learn all the facts, we will have gained true knowledge. If we are primarily minds, what we need most is to get the right ideas in the right slots in our heads. Whether in high school, university, or in an online master class, we assume that learning is solely about how much information and how many ideas we can cram into our brains.

From James K. A. Smith's perspective, the current state of worldview thinking reflects a form of rationalism. Much current discussion and teaching about worldview takes the rationalist approach, agreeing the ultimate goal is to get the right information into our heads and put it in the right places. That's what Smith means when he claims that we treat people as if they are 'brains on a stick.' Our bodies, our practices, and our formation are minimized — what we really need is more and more information.

Rationalism and a rationalist approach in our contemporary world are not limited to education. We see it in what Tara Isabella Burton calls, "techno-utopianism" or the "Californian Ideology" (because of its roots in Silicon Valley tech companies). As a philosophy, it prizes performance, optimization, and perfection, lamenting the frail limitations of the human body (and often working to overcome them). Rationalism has been blended with capitalism to drastically shape our economy and how we view ourselves in this world. Mixed with capitalism, it shows up in our need for our own personal "brand" and our willingness to view even our bodies as an economic resource (monetizing our faces and our free time, participating in side hustles and the 'gig economy').

We see it in the apps we have on our smartphones that seek to help us optimize and streamline our days. The pursuit of wellness and health becomes a drive toward maximum efficiency. A nap might be good after lunch, not because we are humans with bodily limits, but because it will boost our productivity in the afternoon. We care for our bodies so that our minds can work best, not because the body is valuable in itself as a gift from God. Burton describes the Californian Ideology as an alternate contemporary 'gospel' to the social justice movement:

> "If social justice culture located the source of moral evil purely in society, the Californian Ideology locates it in the body: those mortal meat sacks and shifty synapses that keep us from achieving our full and fully rational potential."[10]

The body, for many in our contemporary culture, is not a gift to be received, but an obstacle to be overcome — a "mortal meat sack" to be forced and cajoled into doing what the mind wants.

In their book, *Switch*, Dan and Chip Heath draw from the work of psychologist Jonathan Haidt, describing humans as like someone riding an elephant. Our rational side is the rider and our emotional side is the elephant. For the Heaths, the way to facilitate change (in ourselves or in an organization) is to find a way for the rider to get (or often, trick) the elephant to go where the rider thinks it needs to go. "The weakness of the Elephant, our emotional and instinctive side, is clear: It's lazy and skittish, often looking for the quick payoff (ice cream cone) over the long-term payoff (being thin)...Changes often fail because the Rider simply can't keep the Elephant on the road long enough to reach the destination."[11]

Notice the assumptions hidden in this simple analogy. The rider — our rational, thinking mind — knows what to do and, therefore, should be the one guiding the whole person. Unfortunately, the elephant — our animal-like hungers and emotions — gets in the way. Our bodies, our sensations, our emotions, and our hungers might be the driving forces of our actions (we are riding the elephant after all), but they cannot be trusted to do the right thing. They must be tricked or prodded or otherwise led where the mind believes they need to go.

Even though the Heaths are not positing a theory of how we come to know the world, they share with rationalism the belief that the mind and our thoughts can be trusted, and that our bodies and our hungers are suspect. We see this as a common feature of self-help programs, pop psychology, and books and apps that promise to help us 'hack our lives.' Burton observes that, "the Californian Ideology treats all human beings, regardless of their social context, as autonomous minds trapped in feeble bodies."[12] As a theory of knowledge, this mistrust of the body and experience leads to a profound skepticism about the world.

From the time of Descartes, rationalism has been rooted in a form of skepticism. It began with a mistrust of what we can really know, of what we can trust to learn from the outside world. As Descartes and the rationalists sought to build a new foundation for knowledge, they concluded that our thinking minds were the only thing we could truly rely upon. Even if most people would not share (or even be able to state) this philosophical position, we currently live in a world with a widespread and radical skepticism about knowledge.

With empiricism, we see a breakdown in the unity of any concept of truth. If the only source of knowledge is personal experience and any attempt to broaden or generalize that knowledge is seen as a violence toward 'my story' or 'my experience,' we lose the ability to meaningfully discuss truth. In fact, though we retain the language, we lose the ability to talk about truth at all. We can no longer touch or know a thing, only our personal perceptions of it. We know our experiences, but we cannot know or learn anything *from* or *through* our experiences.

With rationalism, we also see a breakdown in the concept of truth. For the rationalists, truth is about logical consistency, about ideas relating together in a way that makes sense. It is not, however, about ideas actually matching up to the world, because the world, our flesh, and our senses are, at a deep level, untrustworthy.

Bavinck assesses the situation accurately: "In both cases and in both directions, the harmony between subject and object, and between knowing and being, is broken."[13] For Bavinck, both empiricism and rationalism lose the concept of truth. For both, we cannot truly know the world. For the empiricist, we know our sensations and perceptions, but cannot access the thing itself. For the rationalist, we know only the idea because we can have little or no reliable knowledge of the outside world. Both approaches struggle to bridge the gap between our mind and the world. Bavinck sees truth as indispensable for thinking and as the ultimate goal of all disciplined thought (that's what he means when he says 'science').

> "If there is no truth, gone with that, too, is all knowledge and science. The Christian religion thus shows its wisdom primarily in this, that it knows and preserves truth as an objective reality, which exists independent of our consciousness and is displayed by God for us in his works of nature and grace."[14]

For Bavinck, there must be a relationship between the one who knows and the thing that is known. He finds that rationalism and empiricism both sever that relationship by claiming that our knowledge can come only from our perceptions (color, sound, taste, touch, smell, etc.) or from our thoughts and ideas, and never the things themselves. We have no access to a thing itself, only to our perception of or our brain's representation of it. Yet, without the relationship between subject and object, between the one who knows and the thing being known, there cannot be any such thing as knowledge.

The proponents of both rationalism and empiricism assert that their position is 'self-evident.' James K. A. Smith's comments about secularism ring true here: "What pretends to be a "discovery" of the way things are, the "obvious" unveiling of reality once we remove (subtract) myth and enchantment, is in fact a construction, a creation."[15]

In summary, Descartes and his rationalist heirs believe that it is 'just the way things are' that our minds are the only thing we can trust. Empiricists, on the other hand, take it for granted that the only thing we can truly know is what we experience with our senses. It is "obvious" and "self-evident" to both, but neither realizes that there is another way.

CONSISTENTLY INCONSISTENT

Before we get to that "other way" — the way of knowledge held forth in the Christian worldview — we need to acknowledge and address another problem. We don't always choose between empiricism and rationalism. Instead, we often hold both positions simultaneously, albeit in an incoherent way. Few of us are consistent and strict empiricists or rationalists. Most of us grab a bit from both. One moment, we claim that everyone must "live their own truth" or "own their own story or identity" (empiricism). At the same time or moments later, we may drink deeply of the latest in social scientific research through apps designed to maximize our productivity, reduce our brain age, or trick ourselves into losing weight (rationalism).

On its surface, this may seem encouraging: perhaps there is no real fracture in how we come to know things and we can hold it all together — after all, we are giving credence to both thought and experience at the same time. There is a difference, though, between a unified worldview and a collection of ideas we happen to hold at once. Instead of trying to fly half a ship, like Anakin and Obi-Wan, we often try to fly two halves of a broken ship at once, very different from flying a whole ship. With a ship (and with a worldview), the whole really is greater than the sum of its parts.

This inconsistency is more than mere hypocrisy. Instead, our fractured culture is filled with an uncritical embrace of contrary beliefs about the world. Some of this is part and parcel of living in a world of 'remixed' religion and belief more generally. However, Alan Noble makes an important distinction between what he calls our "thick" and "thin" beliefs.[16]

Thick beliefs are those convictions that we have thought through. With thick beliefs, we understand the internal logic behind them, how they look in practice, and their impact on the whole of our life. With a thick belief, we understand what we believe and why we believe it. To a significant extent, this book seeks to help us think through what it means to hold to the Christian faith in the midst of fracture and how Christian worldview can be a healing balm and a firm foundation. In this way, this book is intended to help make our beliefs 'thick.'

Thin beliefs, on the other hand, are those we hold without understanding why. This does not mean the beliefs themselves do not have significant impact on our lives or that they lack depth or even truth. It means, however, that we hold them loosely, without having wrestled with them, without having subjected them to any type of critical evaluation.

One of the great challenges, Noble notes, is that we "hold a strange mixture of thin and thick beliefs, even within the same larger belief system. And the way we express our beliefs to others may make no noticeable distinction between thick and thin beliefs."[17] This blending of thick and thin beliefs — what we believe because we know and understand it and what we believe without knowledge or understanding — leads us to live with an inconsistency far deeper than mere hypocrisy. None of us can live out all our beliefs consistently all the time. However, it seems clear that we no longer even want to.

> "The kind of inner conflict between different beliefs that I am describing is much more intense than standard human hypocrisy. Because we are hyperaware of the endless choice in beliefs, and because we are inclined to hold thin beliefs loosely, our tendency is to form a collection of hodgepodge beliefs about the world — beliefs that would be seen as inconsistent if we were to look closely at them and their implications, but we don't. Or at least we try not to."[18]

And so, many of us hold both to forms of empiricism and rationalism in our daily lives. In some ways and some things, we prioritize and rely on our personal experience or our personal story, disparaging whether any of us can truly know the truth outside experience. In other ways and other things, we give primacy to our mind and to ideas, careful to be certain that we think in the right ways, so that we can have peace, optimize our day, or "hack our life." We are never solely empiricists or rationalists, and can never carry out all the implications of our positions. That does not mean, however, that our beliefs and the resulting fracture of knowledge do not have real consequences in our lives.

Consider worship. Back when I was in college, our local campus ministry had a large worship service every Sunday night. The preaching was outstanding, the music was great, and every service included the celebration of the Lord's Supper. Well over a thousand students would gather, filling the room. Every week, though, something interesting happened. After the first four or five songs (and right before the sermon), many of the students would leave. It happened again after the sermon, before the time of prayer and the Lord's Supper. By the time the service ended, hundreds of students had departed. What was going on? It seemed to me that, for some students, the high point and purpose of the worship service was the sermon. They were there to learn more information. They viewed themselves, in James K. A. Smith's language, as 'brains on a stick,' and saw the appeal or purpose of worship as learning more about the Bible. For them, the goal of worship was to get the right biblical knowledge into their heads. When that part of the service was done, they no longer needed to be there.

For those who left earlier, though, worship was about experiencing closeness to God through singing songs of praise. The soaring feeling of hundreds of voices joined together praising God in song, the intimacy of the act of singing and its ability to draw them near to the Lord — that was worship! Once that part of the service was over — once they had experienced closeness to Jesus — they no longer felt a need to be part of the worship service.

Those college students were more honest about what they actually believe than many of us in the pews. However, the same dynamics are part of all of our churches. The students who left after the songs were participating in a kind of empiricism (whether they knew it or not). Their goal was to have an experience of intimacy with God. Experience mattered most and everything else was either unnecessary or a distraction. The students who left after the sermon, on the other hand, were participating in a kind of rationalism (whether they knew it or not). Their goal was to gain more biblical knowledge — everything else was either unnecessary or a distraction.

Even if no one ever gets up and walks out during a worship service, we can have the same conflicting expectations in our congregations. That can lead to the same questions. What is worship? Is it the experience of singing? Is it the preaching? Is it somehow both? The frequent struggles churches encounter trying to hold this all together makes it clear that the fracture is not just "out there in the world." It faces the church every day as we strive to live lives of faith in a secular world.

CROSS-PRESSURE

It is precisely this secular world that makes the fracture so deep and contributes to the unreflective inconsistency of our lives. We often describe our Western culture as 'secular,' but what exactly does that mean? Charles Taylor draws a distinction between three different types of 'secular' — three different ways that the word is used.[19] In the ancient and medieval world, 'secular' was the opposite of 'sacred.' In this sense, it was about vocation, about which realm you worked in. The priest or monk had a sacred vocation, while the farmer, lawyer, or craftsman worked in a secular field.

In the wake of the Enlightenment, the meaning of 'secular' began to change. 'Secular' began to refer to a neutral, non-religious standpoint. For example, public schools are considered secular because they hold no religious affiliation and stand on (allegedly) neutral ground. Secular politics becomes a place where everyone checks religious convictions at the door and discussion is based on mutually agreed-upon, rational principles. In this form of secularism, religion is relegated to the heart or the private devotions of the individual, but is not welcome in the public, secular sphere. For most of us, this is what we think of when we think of our 'secular society.' Those who fear it believe it cuts religion off from public life and discourse. Those who welcome it, see secularism as a way of moving past the intractable divisiveness that comes with religious debate.

It is in this second form of 'secular' that we see the fracture caused by empiricism and rationalism. As religious belief was removed from public life, knowledge had to be rebuilt on a 'neutral' foundation. The two most prominent options for that new foundation were experience (empiricism) and thinking (rationalism).

There is, according to Taylor, a third form of 'secular,' which more accurately describes our current age. Summarizing Taylor, James K. A. Smith describes this third form of secular as where "religious belief or belief in God is understood to be one option among others, and thus contestable (and contested)."[20] What makes the current age 'secular' is that there are no settled convictions. Even the most strident atheist or committed Christian lives with the possibility, however remote, that they may be wrong. Belief in God is not self-evident in our age, but neither is unbelief. We all know people who believe differently than we do. Whether our beliefs are thick or thin, we hold them all more loosely than generations before. Globalization, the internet, migration, and more have placed us in a world where we see not only the *fact* that people believe differently, but feel the *pressure* of their beliefs (and their presence as believers). That is not just a pressure on what we believe, but on how we believe. Smith and Taylor contend that none of us in the modern West are immune from this phenomenon. We live in a new form of secular world where every belief is contested and everyone feels it.

The result is that we live with what Taylor calls 'cross-pressure.' Belief and unbelief push and pull upon us from many different directions. We feel the strain and we feel the loss. People ache for transcendence, for meaning, for purpose, for something more, even if they do not believe it is there. Believers are haunted by the possibility that there might be nothing more, even if they believe there is. Even when the content of our belief itself is not shaken, the loss of confidence is still experienced as a loss. "All sorts of people feel themselves caught in these "cross-pressures" — pushed by the immanence of disenchantment on one side, but also pushed by a sense of significance and transcendence on another side, even if it might be a lost transcendence."[21]

THE SOLUTION: TRUSTWORTHY KNOWLEDGE

How can we have confidence that we know anything? In this chapter, we have examined the fracture opened up between experience and thinking, between empiricism and rationalism. We have seen how both create a gulf between the knower and the things that can be known. We saw that, with empiricism, we can only know anything through our personal experience — we will never be able to get beyond that to know the thing itself. We can know the sight, smell, taste, and feel of a table, of justice, of beauty, or even of truth, but we cannot reach out and touch those things themselves. In empiricism, concepts are untrustworthy —only our senses can be trusted.

If, instead, we follow the principles of rationalism, we are stuck believing we can only know what we conceive in our minds. We can never get beyond our thoughts, ideas, and concepts to know the things themselves. We can know the idea or principle of justice, beauty, truth (or even a table), but we cannot reach out and touch the things themselves. Our senses (and bodies) are untrustworthy. Only concepts and the things we produce with our minds can be trusted.

Must we choose one or the other? Are we left to grab both positions and try to fly two halves of the ship to safety? Or could there be a whole ship out there, ready and able to fly?

There is. Because God is the Creator, we can know the world reliably through both our senses and our thinking. God made all things and holds all things together. He gives us knowledge of the world he created through the very sense organs and mind that he gave us. There is a correspondence between the knower, the knowledge, and the thing known because they all have the same origin — the creative work of God the Father.

While we will look at the theological convictions that ground this philosophical claim in the next chapter, Bavinck's explanation of the Christian view of knowledge is worth looking at in detail. According to Bavinck, it is "through sensation and representations we possess a trustworthy knowledge of objective reality."[22]

First, "trustworthiness" is a key category for Bavinck. The fact that there may be errors, misperceptions, misrepresentations, or even mistakes in our perception does not mean our understanding is not fundamentally reliable and trustworthy, that we genuinely know objects through our sensations and representations.

> "But in the sensations, the objective world is given to us, and this is recognized and accepted by us, just as we perceive it."[23]

Our sensations may be impure and imprecise. Our senses may be faulty and our subjectivity does influence perception. None of that changes that "in sensations and representations we possess a trustworthy knowledge of objective reality."[24] The charge of the rationalists — that the world of sense perception is not perfect — does not cause the problems they think it does. We can mishear things, we can have problems with our eyes, we can even lose our sense of smell. None of that means that our senses are not reliable sources of knowledge. God gives us knowledge of the world through them.

Second, according to Bavinck, neither sensations nor representations need to be the only type of knowledge. Instead, they may be viewed as two sides of a broader understanding of knowledge. "Sensation" is Bavinck's way of talking about experience. "Representation" is his way of talking about how our minds form concepts. Through both, the world is given to us reliably and knowably. We need both sensation and representation. Concepts without observation are empty, but observations without concepts are blind. Both are necessary if we are ever to know the truth. "Knowledge of truth is possible only if we begin with the fact that subject and object, and knowing and being, correspond to each other."[25] The word "begin" is doing important work in this sentence. All who still believe in truth and science [disciplined study] accept, consciously or unconsciously, that there must be a relationship between what we know and we who know it, that such a relationship is an essential starting point.

> "It is science's task to explain this fact, but if it cannot do this, it will then, on pain of suicide, have to leave the matter untouched. And it will be capable of explanation only if it allows itself to be illumined by the wisdom of the divine word, which sets on our lips the confession of God the Father, the Almighty, Creator of heaven and earth. This confession is not only the first article of our Christian faith but also the foundation and cornerstone of all knowledge and science."[26]

Only the confession of God the Father Almighty, Creator of heaven and earth, can uphold the harmony of subject and object. Organs of our perception are connected to the elements that composed the cosmos by a common origin, the creative work of God the Father. As Al Wolters says, "The fundamental knowability of the creation order is the basis of all human understanding, both in science and in everyday life."[27]

The last part of Bavinck's definition to consider is that sensation and representations give us trustworthy knowledge of *objective reality*. Bavinck believes that there is an objective reality and that we can actually know it. Humans don't create and form the world. We don't create the laws of nature or arrange things according to our categories. "To the contrary, it is the human who has to conform his perception and thinking to God's revelation in nature and grace."[28] Bavinck cites Gustav Portig: "Reality does not have to make itself comply with our reason, but rather, on the basis of the whole experience of the whole age, our thinking must seek to lay bare the metaphysics that God has woven into reality."[29] The world we know is not an invention of our mind — our knowledge is the gift of a creative God.

CONCLUSION

We cannot fly half a ship.

In this chapter, we have sought to explore the two halves of human knowledge after their fracture by the modern world. We saw that neither experience nor thinking alone can cross the gap between us and the world around us. Both break the relationship between those who know and the things that can be known. We saw that the answer is neither to choose one side nor to try and fuse them back together. Instead, the solution is to recover the unified vision of knowledge that comes to us because God is our Creator and the Creator of the world.

In the next chapter, we will look in greater detail at just what the ship of knowledge looks like when it is unified in Christian faith.

CHAPTER 3
IT ALL DEPENDS (ON GOD)
KNOWLEDGE IN A CHRISTIAN WORLDVIEW

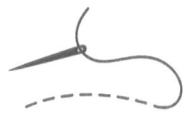

> *"God is not summoned into the presence of reason; reason is summoned into the presence of God."*
> - John Webster

> *"So, in a sense, the answer to the question "Is Christianity true?" is the scandalous reply: "It depends." It depends on the One in whom all things hold together."*
> - James K. A. Smith

In Homer's Odyssey, the intrepid Odysseus seeks to return home after the conclusion of the Trojan War. During one part of his adventure, Odysseus and his crew must pilot their ship through the straits of Messina. On the one side is the six-headed monster, Scylla — most likely a reference to a dangerous rock shoal. On the other side is the deadly whirlpool of Charybdis. It is impossible not to encounter at least one of these monsters and suffer some loss to get through the strait. In the original story, Odysseus is advised to skirt closer to Scylla, losing only a few sailors, rather than lose the whole ship to Charybdis. Odysseus' predicament is the origin of a familiar phrase, "stuck between a rock and a hard place."

Speaking about how we know the world can feel like navigating between twin monsters. On the one hand, we have rationalism, which trusts our mind and our ability to think, but mistrusts our senses. On the other hand, we have empiricism, which mistrusts concepts and only trusts our sense perceptions. Like Odysseus, we often feel like we have only two choices and, whatever we choose, there will be casualties.

But what if this picture of Scylla and Charybdis is the wrong way to view our thinking? As we noted in the last chapter, Bavinck claims that "through sensation and representations we possess a trustworthy knowledge of objective reality."[1] God has created the world to be known and has created us to know it through both our senses and our minds. Instead of navigating between two dangerous beasts, we can actually sail confidently across the ocean. But how? What gives us the confidence that we can truly know the world, that we won't be cast adrift clinging to the boards of our crashed ship?

In this chapter, we will take a closer look at how the doctrine of creation forms the foundation for our ability to know the world. The Christian worldview holds together what our contemporary world has sought to tear apart, including experience and reason, knowledge and character, and even creation and redemption. God created the world to be known and he created us to know it, but God also redeems the world, redeems us, and redeems our ability to know and reflect on the world.

DOCTRINE OF CREATION

God the Creator is the foundation and cornerstone of knowledge. While the modern world has fractured knowledge into experience or reason, into trusting our minds or our bodies, God's creative work enables genuine knowledge of the world and of ourselves. God made the world to be known, made us to know it, and made our minds to grasp the ideas that flow from the wisdom of God.

Ideas and sensation belong together. They are part of a unified understanding of knowledge, because they come from the same source: the creative work of God. God created the world with its sights, tastes, and textures. God also created us with sense organs that can perceive sights, sounds, and smells. The sensations and experience that we have in the world give us reliable knowledge of the world because God gives us knowledge of the world through them. The gap between us (as knowers) and the things that we know is crossed not by our own effort, but by the creative, revelatory, and sustaining work of God. He gives us trustworthy knowledge of the world through the senses he has given us.

In the last chapter, we used the example of a cat crawling into our lap. We experience the sound of the purring, the feel of the weight and warmth of the cat, the sight of it on our lap, and even the feel of its fur as we pet it. Because God has created both the cat and our senses, we can genuinely know that the cat is on our lap. We do not merely have a set of sensations that we group together to conveniently call "a cat on the lap," nor do we simply infer the existence of the cat from that set of sensations. Instead, we have a genuine knowledge of the cat through our senses because God has made our sense organs and the sensations of the world to correspond with one another for the purpose of giving us knowledge. "The law of creation is revelatory: it imparts knowledge."[2]

For the empiricist, what we *know* are our sensations or experience, everything else is conjecture (of one form or another). However, because God is creator, we *know* the cat *through* the sensations. The senses are the means or vehicle of knowledge, not the knowledge itself. "If we perceive the world outside ourselves, then the sensations and representations we receive by it are not the *object* of our knowledge but the knowledge itself, which we have directly obtained through perception of the outside world."[3] Sensations are knowledge or a means of knowledge, but not the object of knowledge. Through sensations we come to know the world around us. We do not deduce an outside world by these sensations (a la Descartes), "which then might not exist or which might exist wholly different from what we perceive."[4]

Our experiences and sensations give us genuine knowledge of the world because that is how God made both us and the world. As Bavinck says, "The doctrine of the creation of all things by the Word of God is the explanation of all knowing and knowing about, the presupposition behind the correspondence between subject and object."[5] In order to know anything, particularly to ever have a discipline of study or body of knowledge, we need there to be a relationship, a "correspondence," between the subject (us) and the object (what we know). This can only be held together because both were created by the one true God and were created to be in relationship with one another.

This does not mean that we always perceive everything correctly, nor that we have complete knowledge or understanding of the world. When I walk through the neighborhood at night and see a medium-sized black animal crossing the road twenty yards away, I might initially think it is a skunk and cross to the other side of the road to avoid it. The fact that I (individually) might be wrong (and it might just have been a possum or stray cat) does not change the fact that our senses (collectively) are generally trustworthy and reliable. More accurately, the fact that we misperceive the world does not mean that God is not clear in his works, but only that we, in our fallen state, cannot hear clearly. "God speaks plainly through his works, but we perversely mishear him."[6]

It is true that physical sensations give us genuine knowledge of the world because God is the Creator, but this is also true of ideas. All things are brought forth from the wisdom of God. God created the world according to the pattern and plan that existed already in the mind of God. As Bavinck says, "The world would not be known to us if it did not exist, but it would not exist if it were not thought of beforehand by God."[7] Before the world existed, it already existed (in some sense) in the mind of God. "We know the things because they are, but they are because God has known them."[8] What this means is that not only are our sensations and sense organs (the physical stuff of this world and our ability to perceive it) created by God, but also the very ideas and concepts in our minds (the "representations" in Bavinck's terms). Ideas and concepts are not simply mental tools we use to group and interpret sensations.

Ideas like justice, beauty, and truth are real because they exist in the mind of God. God's wisdom encompasses not only the physical stuff and pattern of the world he created, but also the universal concepts of the created order. Universals move into our consciousness along the path of sense perception, then through the thinking activity of the mind. "Objective truth is displayed to us in all the works of God's hands, in nature and history, in creation and re-creation."[9] As the Nicene Creed proclaims, God the Father is the creator of all things, of all things visible and invisible. Both the seen world of our senses and the unseen world of ideas are created by our heavenly Father. Hebrews 11:3 says, "By faith we understand that the universe was formed at God's command, so that what is seen was not made out of what was visible." God did not take a lump of matter and simply form the world, but at his command matter came into existence altogether. There was nothing and at the command of God, suddenly there was something — there was creation. That "something" was not formless or independent, but responded to and was shaped by the command of God.

Not only do our sensations and sense organs correspond

because they come from the same Creator, God, but our sensations and our representations (our experience and our thinking) are likewise both vehicles of reliable knowledge because they have the same source: God. The fracture of our modern world — the supposed forced choice of either experience or thinking, either mind or body — comes from a rejection of that common source. By rejecting God, the modern world has rejected the one who holds together all things and makes knowledge possible.

The result is a world where there is no actual order in the world, but where human beings create order by their conceptual frameworks, making sense out of the "kaleidoscope of sensations." Science assumes both an enduring stability to the world and a purpose/order.[10] Knowledge, science, the discipline of learning altogether — all depend upon the foundation of the Christian faith. Apart from the unity of knowledge given by God the Creator, we cannot truly know the world.

As Creator and through creation, God reveals — he imparts knowledge. Al Wolters helpfully states this biblical position: "To sum up, the whole world of our experience is constituted by the creative will and wisdom of God, and that will and wisdom — that is, *his law* — is everywhere in principle knowable by virtue of God's creational revelation."[11] Because God created the world and created us, we can trust both our senses and our mental reflections as reliable ways of gaining knowledge of the world. True knowledge depends on the work of God.

KNOWLEDGE, REFLECTION, AND CHARACTER

Perhaps the most difficult aspect of conversations about 'how we know things' is that these discussions are honest, but artificial. We were learning and knowing the world long before we could philosophize about it. At our mother's breast, we learned that we were loved. As our father read to us, we learned words and sounds. We learned to make the sound "block" when we picked up a certain object and not others. We learned not to grab the dog's tail or eat his food.

We embark on the journey of knowledge, of living in and understanding the world, as part of being human. It is only later — part of the way down the road — that we begin to reflect about what makes it possible for us to be doing what we are doing. We know more than we know and do more than we know. As James K. A. Smith says, recognizing this "requires pushing back against a very bad habit that philosophers have: treating ordinary human beings as if they were all philosophers."[12]

In this way, too, the Christian claim fits with reality as it is, as we find it. Thinking about knowledge is not about trying to prove something before we can start, but about reflecting on how we know and what makes it possible for us to know. All the other explanations fall flat and only the Christian confession makes sense of the full reality. The God who created the world also created us to know it. As Bavinck says, "Here whoever does not want to begin with faith but demands sufficient proofs bars himself from the way of science and has set his foot on the slippery slope of skepticism."[13] All knowledge begins with a certain kind of faith that we can truly know the world. Faith in the knowability of the world is something we have long before we can even begin to doubt it.

The virtues of faith, hope, and love are vital for thinking. We must begin with faith in the knowability of the world because God has created it and created us so that we can know it. Faith in God is also essential, but in many ways the virtue of faith/trust in the realm of knowing is about our capacity to know the world.

Yet, knowing the world properly is not just about our capacity, but about our character. We need hope and love. That is, we need to comprehend the purpose of knowledge and thinking, and cultivate a love for the good, the true, and the beautiful. Not just capacity, but character, matters for thinking well. In his book, *How to Think,* Alan Jacobs reflects extensively on the role of character in thinking well. He notes that there are whole scientific fields dedicated to how the human brain works — how we process information, how we store memory, or how our minds change. However, these discussions neglect a key component: What is thinking actually *for*? As Jacobs says, "We have thought too much in recent years about the science of thinking and not enough about the art."[14] We need character or virtue to direct us to the right ends or purposes if we are to think well. Skill or technique in thinking will only get us so far. Jacobs again:

> "[B]ringing analytical power to bear on a problem is not enough, especially if one's goal is to make the world a better place. Rather, one must have a certain kind of *character*; one must be a certain kind of person, a person who has both the ability and the inclination to take the products of analysis and reassemble them into a positive account, a structure not just of thought but also of feeling that, when *joined* to thought, can produce meaningful action."[15]

For Jacobs, the purpose of knowing is to act. The separation of knowledge from love, thinking from action, epistemology from ethics, impoverishes both. Knowledge needs to be connected to an end, a purpose, in order to be rightly ordered. The difference between mere knowledge and wisdom is character. We need to know who we are, who we are called to be, and what this world is for in order to develop the wisdom to make proper use of the knowledge we have of the world. Neither rationalism or empiricism — as mere (faulty) theories of knowledge — can bring us to love God and our neighbor.

They cannot direct us how to hope or what to love, as these modern solutions focus solely on capacity, ignoring the character necessary for knowledge.

Dr. Ian Malcolm, in the movie *Jurassic Park*, when challenging the scientists who sought to bring back extinct species of dinosaur, captures this modern spirit well, "Your scientists were so preoccupied with whether they could, they didn't stop to think if they should."

We begin all knowledge in faith. We must trust that the world is firm and knowable, and that we have been created with the capacity to know it. God created the world and created us to be able to know it. We live as if this is true long before we can reflect upon it and understand it. However, knowledge also needs hope and love. It needs hope because true knowledge assumes an end, a goal, a purpose for the world and for us in it.

One of the deep flaws of the modern project is that it rejects all ends and purposes for the world, replacing them with mere 'historical processes' or 'development.' It sidesteps the question of what we are to do with the knowledge we gain about the world. By holding together faith, hope, and love as cardinal virtues, along with God as the Creator, the Christian faith provides a framework not only for why we have the capacity to know things, but how that knowledge should direct us into the path of wisdom and a life of faithfulness. By shaping us to love God and our neighbor, our knowledge can produce meaningful action. By calling us to consider the King and his kingdom as the end and purpose of all things, we come not only to know the world as it is in this moment, but to get a glimpse of what the world (and we in relationship to it) will be in the fullness of time. By understanding more deeply something's end or purpose, we come to understand the thing more fully as well. All of this — faith, hope, and love as they relate to knowledge — depends on God.

IT ALL DEPENDS (ON GOD)

At the heart of modernity is the search for an independent foundation of knowledge. When the world seems to shift and change, modernity seeks to provide a firm, unshakeable, objective foundation upon which to build our understanding of the world. In particular, modernity is the search for knowledge that does not depend upon *anything*, but is firm and secure *apart from God*.

Remember Descartes in the previous chapter. He started by doubting everything, stripping away knowledge down to its bedrock. He doubted his senses, doubted whether the outside world existed, and — crucially — doubted whether God existed. He was left with nothing but his own thinking mind and, from there, he sought to recover everything that he had first doubted — including God. However, the doubting of the existence of God was an intentional move. Instead of grounding our knowledge in God, and how he has created the world and revealed himself through creation, Descartes sought to ground knowledge in humanity. At the core of his account of knowledge is the individual, solitary person. For Descartes, there is room for God, but as part of the building, not as the foundation.

While in many ways our culture and thought has moved beyond Descartes over the last five hundred years, we have not left behind his fundamental project: a firm, unshakeable foundation for knowledge *apart from God*. Both empiricism and rationalism are "solutions" created by the desire to have knowledge that does not depend, but is firm and trustworthy. For empiricism, it is our senses and the data we gather from observing the world that form the foundation of knowledge. For rationalism, it is the working of our minds and the flow of logical conclusions that form that foundation. Some in the contemporary world have rejected both solutions in favor of embracing only the initial skepticism of Descartes, calling into question any and all attempts to claim true and reliable knowledge.

Even before the twin errors of empiricism and rationalism attempted to chop up and pull apart knowledge into reason versus experience and mind versus matter, the modern project was already doomed. It was doomed because it failed to see that all knowledge is dependent. In particular, the modern project *started* by rejecting God as the only true foundation of knowledge and then tried to build an edifice of knowledge without him.

In Matthew 7, Jesus concludes his Sermon on the Mount by speaking of two builders. There is a wise man who builds his house on a firm foundation. When the storms and rains come, the house is able to stand because it is founded on rock. Jesus says that everyone who hears Jesus' words and acts on them is like the wise man, building his house on the rock.

But there is also the foolish man. He builds his house on the sand. The house may have appeared fine while the weather was good, but when the storms came, "the winds blew and beat against that house, and it fell — and great was its fall" (Matthew 7:27).

The modern project is a house built on sand. In searching for a firm foundation, it has rejected the one true foundation in God. When the foundation of knowledge is based on "independent, objective" grounds, there is no foundation at all. It makes the house its own foundation, instead of being built upon a foundation. In rejecting the rock to look for something more solid, modernity ends up building only on sand. No matter the rhetoric, neither rationalism nor empiricism can provide a true foundation for knowledge, because they are not the foundation, but are part of the house itself.

In contrast to modernity, Christianity makes the claim that all knowledge, not just religious knowledge, *depends*. It all depends upon God. Without God, we are left with the fractured options of the modern world — empiricism and rationalism — or we must resign ourselves to never being able truly to know anything, which undermines all knowledge and science. The fact that a whole building rests upon a foundation does not make it weaker, but stronger, if the foundation is secure. The building *depends* upon the foundation for its strength, stability, and footing.

Saying that all knowledge "depends" is not to cast away objective truth. Quite the opposite. When truth depends solely upon us — our mind, our senses, our intellect or perception — then it becomes fundamentally subjective and shifting based upon the perspective and experience of the individual or group. To reject God as the foundation of knowledge is to slide into subjectivism. God reveals through his works — in nature and in grace. God the Creator is the foundation of objective truth. Only the unchanging God is strong enough and firm enough to be the foundation of knowledge. All knowledge and science require an objective world and a world we can know. Both the stability of the world (objectivity) and our ability to know it come from God the Father.

Our knowledge depends on God. It is "dependent." Knowledge *depends* on God making the world and making us so we can know it. Knowledge *depends* upon God upholding the world in such a way that we can have consistent and reliable knowledge. Knowledge also *depends* upon God grounding the objective world outside of us. As James K. A. Smith remarks, "So, in a sense, the answer to the question "Is Christianity true?" is the scandalous reply: "It depends." It depends on the One in whom all things hold together."[16]

Behind the fracturing work of modernity in the realm of knowledge are two key theological claims. On the one hand, there is the rejection of God as the foundation of all things. Romans 11:36 says, "For from him and through him and for him are all things." Not all of modernity has moved toward full-fledged atheism, but in rejecting God as the source and foundation of knowledge, the modern project attempts to have life without God, life apart from God. It pursues being and knowing the world as if God does not exist.[17] However, we cannot truly live independent lives, whatever we attempt. We live in the world God has created, and we depend upon God the Creator to know the world. As Bavinck says, "On this Christian standpoint, all autonomy of the human mind falls away, as if it could produce truth out of its own reasons and through its own means."[18]

However, on the other hand, modernity assumes particular claims about sin and salvation. Reason is unfallen and therefore not caught up in the drama of sin and salvation. The Christian claim (usually labelled under the name 'total depravity') is that every aspect and faculty of human life and creation is impacted by sin. There is no area that is cordoned off or left pristine and undamaged by the Fall. Even our minds — how we think, the logic we employ, and how we interpret our senses — have been touched by the Fall. In order to think and know the world, we need not only God the Creator, but we also need God the Redeemer.

THE REDEMPTION OF REASON

One of the reasons for the twin errors described in Chapter 2 is the implicit belief that reason is not impacted by the Fall and, therefore, does not need to be redeemed. Theologian John Webster, in his excellent little book, *Holiness*, argues that reason (or thinking) is caught up in the drama of God's redemption. Like all of creation, reason is fallen and must be redeemed in Christ. However, we have largely bought into the modern belief in untainted, "pure" reason. "Modernity has characteristically regarded reason as a 'natural' faculty — a standard, unvarying and foundational feature of humankind, a basic human capacity or skill. As a natural faculty, reason is, crucially, not involved in the drama of God's saving work; it is not fallen, and so requires neither to be judged nor to be reconciled nor to be sanctified."[19]

Reason is implicitly seen in the modern world as outside of the influence of sin. It is perfect — perfectly rational and therefore perfectly objective, clear, and unsullied by the messiness of human life. History, humanity, or the soul might need redemption, but reason does not. "Once reason is thought of as 'natural' rather than as 'created' (or, to put it differently, once the category of 'the created' is collapsed into that of 'the natural'), then reason's contingency is set aside, and its sufficiency is exalted in detachment from the divine gift of truth."[20] The use of the term "natural" instead of "created" is crucial for understanding Webster's point. When we speak in terms of creation, we are speaking theologically. We speak with an eye and ear to the great drama of Creation, Fall, and Redemption. However, to change this language to "nature" is to speak of something static and unmoving, something that has always been this way and does not change. "Creation" is caught up in the work of redemption, but "nature" is unmoved and untouched. For Webster, the move to talk of reason as a "natural capacity" makes reason no longer dependent on God (or anything else), but also sets it outside the drama of salvation.

The scriptures tell a different story about reason and thinking than the one told in the modern world. Romans 1:18-20 says,

> "The wrath of God is being revealed from heaven against all the godlessness and wickedness of people, who suppress the truth by their wickedness, since what may be known about God is plain to them, because God has made it plain to them. For since the creation of the world God's invisible qual-

ities—his eternal power and divine nature—have been clearly seen, being understood from what has been made, so that people are without excuse."

According to this passage, God has clearly revealed his power and his divine nature since the beginning of creation. From creation, we can know God's power and nature. However, because of our wickedness, we suppress the truth. That is, there is a gap between what is revealed and what is perceived. God shows himself clearly in his works, but we do not see him clearly, because we actively turn away from and push down the truth.

In some ways, this is the very story of the modern project and why it has led to such fractures in our contemporary world. However, for the purposes of thinking about "reason," it is important to note that our thinking and perceiving of God is clearly impacted by sin. In the context of Paul's argument in Romans, this passage points out how all people (and, indeed, every part of us) are fallen into sin and deserving of wrath. This is not a result of any fault of God or God's revelation — the fault lies with us. We turn reason into a weapon to reject the truth of God.

Modernity claims that reason need not be redeemed, for it never fell in the first place. Webster, rightly, refuses to oblige modernity. "Christian theology, however, must beg to differ. It must beg to differ because the confession of the gospel by which theology governs its life requires it to say that humankind in its entirety, including reason, is enclosed within the history of sin and reconciliation...reason, no less than anything else, stands under the divine requirement that it be holy to the Lord its God."[21]

God's claim upon the world includes a claim upon reason. Reason is summoned to stand before God, which means that reason must be redeemed and sanctified. When God promises to set all things right and make all things new, to renew a groaning and bound creation, that promise includes the created faculty of reason. "One of the grand myths of modernity has been that the operations of reason are a sphere from which God's presence can be banished, where the mind is, as it were, safe from divine intrusion. To that myth, Christian theology is a standing rebuke."[22]

This redemption of reason will follow the same pattern as all of redemption: dying and rising. For reason to be made holy — to be able to serve the holy God as it was created to do — it must first die to any form of life apart from God. The autonomy, the self-service, the drive for independence that characterizes human life, and human reason as an aspect of that life, must be buried in Christ to rise again in him. "Holy reason is mortified reason. It is reason which has been judged and destroyed as it has been set under the judgment of God against what Paul calls 'all ungodliness and wickedness of men who by their wickedness suppress the truth' (Rom 1.18)."[23] The God who judges reason, who rebukes it for suppressing the truth of God's revelation, is the same God who rescues reason. Reason as an independent "natural faculty" that can go its own way and serve its own ends must die so that it can be raised to serve the purpose God made it — and all creation — for: to glorify God. As Webster says, "Reason is holy because God acts upon reason, arresting its plunge into error and freeing it from its bondage to our corrupt wills and our hostility to God. And to describe theological work as a work of holy reason is to say that without talk of this God and his acts of judgment and renewal, we cannot depict what happens when we take it upon ourselves to venture the work of the theologian."[24] Independent reason must die so that it can be given life again by the sanctifying and merciful work of the living God.

CONCLUSION

Each of us begins life learning about the world around us. We learn touch, tastes, and sounds. We learn words and concepts and think through consequences and possibilities. But at some point down our road of learning, a question might begin to surface: *how do I actually know what I know?*

We can know the world because God has made the world to be known and made us to be able to know it. The harmony or correspondence between us (the knowers) and what we know is grounded in God the Creator. Apart from God the Creator, knowledge falls apart and we are left with the fractures of our contemporary world — empiricism and rationalism. However, though God's creative work gives us trustworthy knowledge of the world, even our reason and our senses are caught up in the drama of salvation. We often misperceive the world and our reason can be flawed and faulty. We might have a plethora of information but lack the character or wisdom to bring that knowledge into meaningful action. God reveals himself clearly through creation, but in our sin, our ears cannot hear and our eyes cannot see. All this points to the need for God to be not only our Creator, but also our Redeemer.

The need for the redemption of knowledge indicates why the Christian worldview is more than simply a "theistic" worldview. We cannot have knowledge without God as Creator. But because of our condition, it is not enough. True knowledge can only be possible if that God also redeems and saves, also puts to death our sinful character and twisted reason, and also raises them both from the grave.

CHAPTER 4
LIFE FINDS A WAY

CHANGE AND STABILITY IN THE MODERN WORLD

> *"It is only when we exchange the mechanical and dynamic worldview for the organic that justice is done to both the oneness and diversity, and equally to being and becoming."*
> - Herman Bavinck

> *"There are more things in heaven and earth, Horatio, than are dreamt of in your philosophy."*
> - Hamlet, Prince of Denmark

Anna and Olaf dance through the leaves singing, "some things never change." After the harrowing events of *Frozen*, the sequel opens with two of the characters wishing and hoping that life has finally settled down and that they can find some stability. The joyful chorus about certainty and changelessness runs contrary to the verses and to the scenery around them as they sing. They want nothing to change, but it will. How can they feel safe and secure when change (sometimes good and sometimes bad) seems inevitable? Walls crumble, relationships change, people grow, and Peter Pumpkin becomes fertilizer.

One of the big dilemmas we all face, whether as fictional

characters in a Disney movie or as humans approaching adulthood or old age, is change. The world seems stable, rational, and secure, and yet everything around us changes. Even we, ourselves, change as we grow and age. How do we make sense of change and account for the general stability and consistency of the world around us?

Both historically and in our contemporary world, many have settled into one of two responses to change in the world: either change is the constant and the stability of the world is an illusion, or the opposite is true. As we will see in this chapter, both positions have long histories and very present manifestations. Yet, both options have deep problems rooted in their rejection of the God revealed in Scripture. Only a recovery of God as Creator and the world as creation (and not simply "the universe") can help us make sense of our world.

TWO ANCIENT POSITIONS: MATERIALISM AND DYNAMISM

Though the question of how to understand change takes on a specific character in our contemporary world, the question is as old as philosophy itself. Among ancient philosophers, there were only two positions, which stood in direct opposition to one another.

The first position, materialism, holds that matter is real and permanent, but change and movement are a facade. Matter is all there is. Time and space are merely subjective ways of thinking. There is no need (nor is there any room) for an account of the soul or for other transcendent matters. In classic accounts, even the possibility of change or movement can be challenged.

The most famous way of describing this position comes from the ancient philosopher Zeno of Elea. Zeno asks a series of questions, which he believes demonstrate that motion and change, contrary to our senses, are impossible. If a runner takes 20 seconds to run 100 meters, how long does it take him to run half that distance? 10 seconds. What about half that distance? 5 seconds. Half again? 2.5 seconds. He goes on, but the point is that you always have to arrive halfway to somewhere before you get the whole way there. But if this is true, how is it possible to ever start? To move at all requires moving through an infinite amount of 'halfway points,' which is impossible. Throughout the centuries, there have been numerous rebuttals to "Zeno's paradox," but at the heart of Zeno's claim is that motion is impossible. There is only matter, no change. Nothing becomes anything else: everything simply *is*.

The second position, dynamism (named from the Greek word for energy or power), holds that change (or 'becoming') is real and that matter and permanence are a facade. Under this approach, the only constant is change itself. People and, indeed, the universe itself are in a constant process of contradiction. Like someone peddling a bike or paddling a kayak, the constant back and forth propels the universe forward and leads to change and development. Motion is constant and we are always changing all the time.

For the dynamists, this is true not only of human nature, but of the world around us. The idea that a wooden chair simply *is* a chair is nothing more than an idea. It is a chair now, but before it was a bunch of boards and screws. Before that it was a tree in the forest and iron ore in the ground. Later, it will rot in a landfill and become soil, which will someday transform into something else. Nothing stays the same. The only constant is change.

These ancient schools of thought have taken on new forms in our contemporary world. The philosophical questions about being and becoming, matter and change, are still being asked and must still be answered. The scientific questions about the relationship of matter and energy are still before us.

Bavinck remarks that materialism and dynamism are on opposite sides of this question: "While materialism regards matter as an eternal substance and energy as pertaining to it, dynamism, on the contrary, sees energy as original and material as derivative."[1] However, the most pressing questions in our day are not about change itself or about quantum physics, but about the relationship between God and the world, about whether transcendence can exist in a world that seems governed by natural laws. How can it be possible to believe simultaneously in miracles and natural laws, to believe simultaneously in the soul and in science?

Between the two sides of materialism and dynamism, some thinkers have sought a mediating position. In particular, "atomism" tries to explain the world "from a mechanism of immutable, material, soulless atoms."[2] Atomism does not have the same problems with change as materialism does, but it shares similar core convictions. With atomism, matter is all there is. There is no need to speak of the soul, the spiritual, or God. But atomism differs in that it can speak of motion and change. Everything can be explained through cause and effect, by way of the natural laws of physics and natural science. The world is like a machine filled with many tiny parts (atoms) that interact to bring the universe to its current state. When we understand all the parts and how they interact, we understand the world.

Following Bavinck, we will refer to this modern form of materialism and atomism as 'mechanism.' Mechanism treats the world like a machine. This position existed in the ancient world — it has come to dominate the spirit of our times.

MODERN MECHANISM: THE DRIVE FOR EFFICIENCY

Mechanism is by far the dominant perspective in our culture. Searching for explanation through cause and effect, taking a close and detailed look at atoms, at systems, at small and large parts and then detailing their interactions, formulating hypotheses, and stating natural laws — this approach has been a great boon for civilization and culture. It has led to cures for many diseases. It has put a man on the moon. It has helped us see things about our world and about ourselves that we would not have otherwise seen. The ability to focus and look at the world through a mechanical lens has generated much good in our world.

However, the problem arises when mechanism becomes the *only* lens through which we view the world. When we take everything in our world and cut it up into its smallest parts, we lose something. When we view everything as a machine with all its tiny parts, we miss so much. As the saying goes, when you are a hammer, everything looks like a nail. In a culture dominated by mechanism, every area of life and the universe becomes another opportunity to dissect and examine.

One of the ways this mechanism shows up in contemporary life is in the perpetual drive for efficiency. Alan Noble puts it succinctly (efficiently?), "That's not to say that we never prioritize other values — we certainly do — but our one agreed-upon value in nearly every sphere of life tends to be efficiency."[3] It is everywhere and always assumes that if we can do a good thing, we do it even better if we do it more efficiently. We constantly tweak the machines of business, government, schools, or even churches in order to get the same output with less input (or better results with the same initial cost).

In fact, I remember learning once that a company/church/organization's core values are best defined by what it would do regardless of its impact on the bottom line. Our default is that the most efficient is best. Only in rare instances where it touches "core values" would we ever think of ignoring efficiency (and maybe not even then, as it turns out). We have conferences and seminars about boosting productivity in the workplace. We hear (and sometimes make) regular complaints about the inefficiency of government bureaucracy. Schools face constant pressure to improve their scores on standardized tests without increasing the number of hours with students.

Many of these concerns are valid and many of these adjustments might be good. However, when efficiency moves from *one* of our values to the *single* value we all can agree to follow, it gets distorted. As Alan Noble says, "Efficiency has many healthy applications when it is not treated as an *ultimate* good."[4] The problem is that efficiency does not easily tolerate other values or considerations. It pushes out or dominates every other concern. It might be great to boost test scores or college admittance rates, but when the concern for efficiency causes us to ignore the way these methods harm students, something is wrong. It might be more efficient to produce the same shirt for less money and increase profit margins, but when efficiency ignores the basic needs of the very person who made the shirt or produced the materials for it, something is wrong.

Efficiency and mechanism both view human beings as machines. The same approach to improve the fuel mileage on the newest model Toyota is applied to increase the mileage on the current model of Fred and Sandra and Andre. The same microscope lens we use to examine E. Coli, we now turn on Edward. We employ the same methods (examine the parts, see how they interact) and the same goals (increase production or efficiency) to view all parts of our life and our world.[5]

But people are not machines. Yes, we have muscles and bones and internal organs — we have parts that can be examined and much can be learned about them. Yes, it is possible to study human behavior or psychology, to examine how groups work together, to consider the dynamics of power and belonging, to learn how people change their minds and how to best influence others. It is possible to learn all these things and more by looking at people through a mechanistic lens.

But not everything in the universe is a nail. The lens of

cause and effect, of detailed study and disciplined examination is good. But the mechanistic approach (seen in our obsession with efficiency) has come to dominate how we view *everything* in the contemporary world.

One of the deep and unsettling facets of mechanism is that it denies any transcendence. Cause and effect, the smallest parts, the systems, and how they interact — these things provide our total explanation for the universe. They are not merely one part of the explanation, but the whole account. The world is all there is and we are all just a bunch of atoms, molecules, and synapses firing in our brains.

However, as James K. A. Smith points out, "'We moderns' are not entirely comfortable with modernity."[6] We feel the sense that something has been lost when the world is reduced to all its parts, cut into tiny bits. The person who dissects a fish may end up learning a lot about how it is able to live, and about its internal structure and organs, but by the time the dissection is done, the fish is dead. In a similar way, we get the feeling that, though we may learn much from diagramming, dissecting, and examining the world in all its smallest parts, something dies when that is the only way we view the world.

Humans are made for transcendence, so we search for it anyway. Far from the rise of mechanism causing the decline of religion or a belief in the spiritual or transcendent, it has coincided with a rise in what we have referred to as "remixed religion." We do not easily live in a world without perceived meaning or purpose or wonder. This reaction to the problems of mechanism has led to an opposite error: the rise of a new form of dynamism.

SEND VIBES PLEASE

Jurassic Park is supposed to be completely safe. An amusement park full of once extinct dinosaurs, the whole park is completely safe, explains John Hammond, its founder. The animals cannot get out and cannot even reproduce. Geneticists have ensured that every dinosaur on the island is female. Dr. Ian Malcolm, who has been brought in to vet the park, is incredulous. According to Malcom, the park managers pretend they are in control, but they are dealing with powers beyond their control. "Life breaks free, it expands to new territories, and crashes through barriers painfully, maybe even dangerously, but, uh, well, there it is," Malcolm says. John Hammond dismisses Malcolm's concerns, contending that, "Creation is an act of sheer will." But Malcolm is insistent, "Life will find a way."[7]

The book and the movie show Malcolm ultimately to be right. The dinosaurs break free, the park gets out of control, people are killed and eaten, and — wonder of wonders — the dinosaurs are breeding. But Malcolm's objections to the park are not simply about the myth of human control or even a belief in the superiority of dinosaurs. They don't arise because he has a theory about how the animals could reproduce if they are all female. No, they stem from his belief in the power of life itself. Species may come and go, individual humans and animals will be born and die, but Life will grow and continue. Life, as he says, will find a way.

The fictional Malcolm shares some very real-world beliefs with a growing set of people in our contemporary culture. Though his claims are framed in the language of science and objectivity (Malcolm is a world-renowned mathematician, after all), there is something almost mystical about his claims. His belief in life, in the power of life, in the permanence and resilience of life even in the face of death and extinction, has a religious fervor and tone. Life — with a capital L — will find a way. It is a power, a force, which is beyond us, and which cannot ultimately be denied.

Mechanism, with its belief in strict causes, firm matter and rules, and with its denial of the transcendent, remains the dominant way of understanding the world in the contemporary West. However, a growing number of people believe a form of dynamism more akin to the ideas of Dr. Ian Malcolm than its ancient forms. Even a hundred years ago, Herman Bavinck noted a shift taking place within the scientific community. The concept of a "life force" was coming back into favor among biologists. Some biologists were beginning to reject strict materialism and claim that the most essential properties of life cannot be grasped by the natural sciences.[8] In other words, Hamlet is making a comeback. "There are more things in heaven and earth, Horatio, than are dreamt of in your philosophy."[9] The world is bigger than science can see.

Dynamism, however, has moved out of the laboratory and the lecture hall and into the marketplace. Your aunt may not be thinking about whether it is possible for change to exist in a stable world, but she will ask for everyone to send "prayers and positive vibes" her way in anticipation of her upcoming surgery. Your neighbor may not be concerned about whether matter or energy are primary in the universe, but he is on that new superfood regime that promises to clear his body of toxins, and he has rearranged the furniture in his room so that the space has different energy. This new, contemporary dynamism shows itself in the growing belief in 'spiritual energy' and has its most powerful form in contemporary wellness culture.

In her research on American 'remixed' religion, Tara Isabella Burton observes that language that was once associated with New Age or New Thought has now become mainstream. In a world made flat by mechanism, many still search for meaning and transcendence. "The language of energy, toxins, adaptogens, and neuron velocity — so much of it rooted in flawed or outright fallacious science — is also about providing us with a sense of meaning, of order."[10] Just as romanticism was a reaction against the cold rationalism of previous generations, the wellness and spiritualist movements of today are a reaction to the lonely, meaningless world painted by mechanism. However, these contemporary forms seek not to reject science, but to co-opt its language and authority in order to sell a product, a vision, or a lifestyle.

For the new dynamists, people, places, and things all have energy. There is a power, a spiritual force, a connection between things. "Energy — something that is at once spiritual, metaphorical, and scientifically concrete — runs through us all."[11] As self-described "soul coach," Jakki Smith-Leonardini, puts it, "Everything is made of energy and has its own unique vibration, including you."[12]

These are not new ideas. In the past people believed that matter itself was in some sense alive or that the universe had a mind, a soul, or a consciousness.[13] It is not even new to make spiritual and metaphysical claims and frame them in the language of pure science and observation. The difference with contemporary dynamism, though, is how widespread the belief is and how easily it sells. As Burton notes, teaching about "energy" is no longer a fringe belief. "Americans are increasingly taking this seriously. In 2018, a full 42 percent of Americans said they believed that "spiritual energy can be located in physical things." Those numbers were highest among the "unaffiliated" (47 percent) and, more specifically, the "nothing in particular" (61 percent). But Christians said they shared this ideology too. Thirty-seven percent of self-identified Christians also said they believed in "energy.""[14]

We see it when people ask us to send them "prayers and vibes" or "positive energy" before a job interview, as if prayers to the Creator and positive thoughts directed toward the person are equivalent activities. We also see it in the blending of spirituality and pseudo-science in much of the health and wellness movement. We cleanse ourselves of toxins, remove what doesn't spark joy, or try to align our selves (or our souls) in the right direction. And at every turn, there is a product for us to buy or a seminar for us to attend.

While mechanism seeks to cut everything into its smallest pieces, dynamism seeks to connect everything together. Mechanism cuts the fish up to see its organs. Dynamism wants to see a living fish swim. For mechanism, the diversity of the universe is paramount. For dynamism, unity is key.

Dynamism, at least in its contemporary forms, lives as a reaction to the cold, lifeless mechanism of the modern world. It is a resistance to the narrowing of the world and to the cutting off of the transcendent and mysterious. Dynamism sheds valuable light on the insufficiency of mechanism, but it has its own equally serious objections to face. Neither mechanism nor dynamism can take the world as it truly is. Either option ends up pulling the world apart at the seams.

UNITY *OR* DIVERSITY: THE PROBLEMS WITH DYNAMISM AND MECHANISM

Neither mechanism nor dynamism can make full sense of the world as it truly is. Each favors one aspect of creation and cuts off the other. Both face significant challenges that are only truly met by the worldview presented in Scripture.

First, mechanism cannot account for life itself. According to Bavinck, objections to mechanism (within the scientific community) have come primarily from the field of biology. The deeper the research into the fundamental nature of life, the more of a mystery life becomes. "Despite all the progress of science...the rift between the lifeless and the living nature of life, rather than being filled, only became broader and deeper."[15] The gap between the living and non-living only grows larger, the more we learn. We can break down the complex life forms into smaller and smaller parts, learning more and more along the way, but the sheer difference between lifeless matter and a living organism remains profound.

In an ironic twist on Zeno's paradox, the challenge is no longer how change is possible, but how life is possible. No matter how much we break down the pieces of a living being, there must be that first step across the threshold from non-living to living. Mechanism cannot explain it. The "we are all just a bunch of atoms bouncing around" theory doesn't provide an adequate explanation of reality. It might *possibly* be able to account for how matter coalesced into the forms it does today, but it cannot explain how this group of atoms and molecules is truly and wonderfully *alive*.

Second, in mechanism, there is a shift in imagination regarding nature. We no longer easily imagine ourselves living in a "cosmos," but in a "universe."[16] In the past, nature was a broad category that encompassed all of creation — the physical and the spiritual. However, mechanism redefines nature merely as "the natural." It equates nature with the purely physical, with the things that mechanism is good at measuring and explaining. When we limit nature to the purely physical, it makes sense that the mechanical explanation exists. However, it takes one aspect of nature and equates it with all of nature. It also applies the method that works there to every other phenomenon in existence. This is its greatest problem. Mechanism is really good at hammering nails, so it not only views everything in the world as a nail, but denies that anything but nails actually exist. "In [mechanism], nature is simply identified with the world of physical phenomena, and the mechanical explanation [of the world] is exalted as the only scientific explanation, whatever goes beyond it is supernatural, a miracle, and miracles are naturally impossible!"[17] Mechanism only allows one form of explanation for everything in creation.

However, dynamism has its own share of problems, too. What does it mean to say that "spiritual energy" is real? We know push and pull, tone and color, movement and change. This is different than claiming that there is an objective reality to these energies. While Bavinck delves deeply into the science and philosophy of his time (around 100 years ago), the increased appeal of dynamism today is largely unscientific and unphilosophical.[18] It is not so much that people are convinced of "spiritual energy" by a scientific or rational proof as that they themselves are disenchanted by the disenchanted vision of the contemporary world.

Contemporary dynamism attempts to grasp at transcendence and the fundamental unity of all things in a world that has broken apart. It hungers to see life and the universe as a living thing, instead of a cold dead fish on the laboratory table. In some of these impulses, contemporary dynamism touches the truth. The simple (or complex) causal explanations of the world can be transcended. But what transcends is not a something — it is a someone. It is not that there is an energy or life-force operating in the universe — there is a God who created all things, who is both above and wholly other than his creation and who actively sustains and guides it. Contemporary dynamism is right to insist on transcendence, but it ultimately gravitates toward either pantheism (the belief that God is all things and all things are God) or panentheism (the belief that God is *in* all things). Dynamism looks out at the mechanistic world and believes there must be more to it than that. The "more" that they look for in the universe is a power and not a person.

There is a unity and connection to all things. A person is not simply a collection of atoms and molecules, but a *person*. There is a fundamental unity to all of the universe, but this stems not from a shared energy or power, but because it all comes from the same source. All of creation exists as a result of the creation of the one God. The unity of the various parts of creation is rooted in the God who created them.

There is an energy, a creative and purposeful movement to the world. It is not that the world is comprised of energy or that life as a power or force must move forward ("life finds a way"), but that the world was created by God. God, the living God, gives life to the fish and birds, animals and plants, and gives them the ability to produce more of their own kind. The power for life to make life comes from the hand of the living God. Creation has a creative purpose, because it was created *for* a purpose. Creation moves toward an end or goal, not as a result of purely natural processes, but because of the guiding and sustaining work of God.

For all its strengths — in rejecting mechanism's breaking of the world into all its parts and in calling instead for a re-emphasis on the transcendent and unity of the world — contemporary dynamism ultimately leads to a break between matter and energy, between the physical and the spiritual. Dynamism simultaneously blends matter and spirit and pulls them apart. Dynamism either rejects the rules and explanations of mechanism altogether, or it claims that the spiritual and material operate under different rules. Dynamism can hold fast to its claim that everything changes and that the only constant is change, thereby rejecting the rules and explanations of mechanism. In doing so, however, it undermines the entire project of disciplined learning and makes all knowledge impossible (not just scientific knowledge). Without a stability to creation, it becomes impossible to know the world with any confidence or reliability. However, if dynamism grants mechanism its authority over the physical world, but claims the spiritual realm operates by different rules (energy, toxins, vibes, karma, etc.), then it leads to a break between matter and spirit. While it intends to draw a deeper connection between the spiritual and physical, between the world and god,[19] it actually does the opposite. Spirit and matter coexist in this world, but they are not alike, they do not belong together. Two laws, two sets of rules, two incompatible explanations for reality serve to drive them apart instead of bringing them together.

UNITY *AND* DIVERSITY: THE ORGANIC WORLDVIEW

The way forward is to recover an organic view of the relationship between God and the world, between stability and change, between unity and diversity. As we have stated before, the solution to the problems of modernity is not to find a compromise or some mediating position between the extremes, but to knit back together the fabric that the modern world has sought to tear apart. Just as many Christians held a "worldview" long before the word was used, many Christians also viewed the world "organically" long before the word was used. Drawing from Bavinck, we are using the word "organic" in a very specific sense. We will use it to refer to the unity and diversity of creation as it has been created, formed, and directed by the Triune God. In the next chapter, we will spend more time fleshing out the meaning of "organic," looking at its roots in the biblical witness, and considering its implications for our life in this world. First, however, it will be helpful to briefly note two aspects of the organic worldview as its contrasts to both mechanism and dynamism.

First, the organic worldview is teleological. That means that creation has a purpose, an end (*teleology* comes from the word *telos*, Greek for 'end/goal/purpose'). The change inherent in the world is not the result of random fluctuations. Instead, creation becomes what God has designed it to be (and what he is providentially guiding it to be). Sin and the will of sinful creatures can work against that purpose, but the creation itself is fundamentally purposeful, in stark contrast to mechanism (and much of dynamism). Scientific and mechanical explanations of the world can explain what something does, how it changes over time, or even name its various parts, but they cannot explain what something is *for*.[20] Part of the narrowness of mechanism (and why it feels so bleak to many) is that it lacks the ability to answer "why?" If we ask why there is a violin, mechanism can explain where it comes from, the process of tree growth and harvesting, the craftsmanship that goes into making a violin, the types of sounds it produces (and the accompanying vibrations), but it cannot truly tell you what a violin is *for*, its purpose. Where something comes from and how it is made do not constitute a full explanation of the thing. The organic worldview contains within it a strong emphasis on purpose because God created the world. God, in his wisdom, made the world, so it has a nature and a destination which drives its development.

Second, the organic worldview has a fuller understanding of nature than mechanism or dynamism. Nature in Christianity is a bigger and richer concept than what is seen in most natural science. "*Nature* encompassed the entirety of creation, the spiritual as well as the material."[21] When Christian theology speaks of "nature", it is usually limited to the creature and creation, but not simply to the natural world. It also refers to spiritual creation. Angels, the soul, and heaven are all part of "nature," because all are part of the creation of God. Originally Christians talked of spiritual nature and corporeal nature, physics of the body and physics of the soul. It was one field of study with two parts. There were distinctions between those two parts, but also a fundamental unity to the study because they had the same source (God) and were part of the same world. Even when physics became more associated with the physics of the body, there was still the study of *pneumatica* — doctrine of God, angels, and the soul (*pneuma* being the Greek word for "spirit"). "But slowly nature and *physica* have acquired a far narrower meaning; nature now usually refers only to "the perceptible external and that which is set in opposite to the spirit," and *physica* has become the science of molecular movements, the doctrine of the laws that obligingly appear in lifeless nature."[22] Basically, nature, or "physics," used to refer to body and soul, to physical and spiritual creation, but has been reduced in modern times to apply only to the merely physical phenomena of the world.

When we limit nature to the purely physical, then it makes sense that the mechanical explanation exists. However, mechanism takes one aspect of nature and equates it with *all* of nature. Mechanism applies the method that works with physical reality to every other phenomenon in existence. "Soul and life, consciousness and freedom, spirit and thought are just as much phenomena as matter and force are in nature as we perceive them, and they have a right to be explained."[23] The organic worldview recovers the whole vision of nature as body and soul, as physical and spiritual, and seeks to treat both adequately and coherently. "It does not approach nature with a theory but rather takes it as it gives itself to us."[24]

As we will explore in greater depth in the next chapter, the organic worldview holds together what the modern world tries to tear apart. And it does so, not primarily on the basis of philosophical speculation, but on the revelation of God. "The full truth is first presented to us in Holy Scripture, which teaches that things have come forth from God's "manifold wisdom," that they are mutually distinguished by a common character and name, and that in their multiplicity they are one, and that in their unity they are still distinct."[25]

CONCLUSION

Only an organic worldview can make sense of the world as it is. The worldview held forth in the Bible holds together the stability of the world and change by recognizing that the unchanging God made both the physical and spiritual world and made it with a purpose. He leads and guides its change as it develops towards fulfilling its destiny. Mechanism — viewing the world as a machine with various parts — is good at explaining many things, but often oversteps its place and tries to explain everything as if it was a clock with small turning gears. Dynamism — the reactionary opposite of mechanism — appeals to life and energy and forms of spiritualism to find meaning and transcendence, but rejects or subverts our ability to know true things about the world.

Both seek to impose an order on a world they often believe, at heart, lacks meaning and purpose. The rejection of God that lies at the heart of the modern project leaves people to experience a world they believe is devoid of purpose, of hope, of a defined future.

For many Christians, the rise of mechanism and dynamism is seen as a threat, as something to bewail and despair. However, perhaps we should look at these perspectives as an opportunity. The people clamoring for crystals or cleansing themselves of toxins hunger for a world with meaning, for a life that is more than just eating and sleeping over and over again until we die. Into this restless void, the church can present a better, truer account of the world, one with hope and a future found in Jesus Christ. The same is true for those searching for control or security through rational and scientific explanations. The church can speak a better and more beautiful truth, extolling a firmer foundation in Jesus Christ.

Remember, a worldview is a needle. It can be used to pop a balloon or remove a splinter, but its purpose, what it is *for*, is mending and sewing back together that which has been torn apart. As we see people in our world struggling with the fraying of contemporary life (and even feel that ourselves), may we hold forth the full fabric of our faith and seek to sew together what has begun to tear.

CHAPTER 5
CERTIFIED ORGANIC

CHANGE AND STABILITY IN A CHRISTIAN WORLDVIEW

> "In Christ, in the middle of history, God created an organic centre; from this centre, in an ever widening sphere, God drew circles within which the light of revelation shines."
> - Herman Bavinck

> "God does not make junk, and we dishonor the Creator if we take a negative view of the work of his hands when he himself takes such a positive view."
> - Al Wolters

"What is it?" That first morning in the wilderness, when "thin flakes like frost on the ground appeared on the desert floor" (Ex 16:14), Israel did not know what to make of it. They eventually called it manna (from the words "what is it" in Hebrew), but the question was genuine. "What is it?" could have been answered by explaining where the bread came from. It came from heaven. God gave it to them. "What is it?" could have been answered by explaining its composition and how it worked. It was bread. It would fall every day but the Sabbath. The Israelites were to collect an omer (about 2 quarts) for each person in their tent, except twice as much on the day before the

Sabbath. But "what is it" could also have been answered by explaining its purpose. This bread was for eating. It was the means God gave the Israelites to sustain them in the wilderness. All three explanations are true and all three together make much more sense of manna than any single explanation.

One of the challenges we face in our contemporary world is that we have limited the answers we accept to the question "what is it?" Mechanism and dynamism offer mutually exclusive answers to the question. In doing so, they cut us off from seeing the world as it actually is. We need to know where things come from, what they are, and what they are for in order to properly understand our world. We need to recover an organic worldview.

In this chapter, we will explore in greater depth what Bavinck means when he speaks of the Christian worldview as "organic." We will also see how Bavinck's use of the word "organic" differs from many popular uses of the word. Next, we will look at how God's wisdom provides the structure and stability of creation, but also accounts for its development. We will then look at how mechanism fails to account for development and why we need to recover the purpose of creation. Lastly, we will argue that we need a renewal of worship, far more than books, in order to recover a Christian view of the world.

CERTIFIED ORGANIC?

When Bavinck speaks of the Christian worldview being "organic," he is using the word in a very specific sense. He is not saying that the universe develops 'organically' (in the common usage of the word), that it is free from pesticides or additives. Instead, 'organic' refers to the way God, in creating the world, made it full of unity and diversity. There is a connection and order to the creation, and yet creation also multiplies with distinct and unique beings. Not only protons, electrons, and neutrons, but flamingos, toucans, sparrows, and whippoorwills. Human nature is united and yet diverse as well.

Dynamism treats connection and unity, but cannot explain diversity. Mechanism speaks of the diversity of existence, but cannot make sense of how things are connected. "There are lifeless and living, inorganic and organic, inanimate and animate, unconscious and conscious, material and spiritual creations, which differ, respectively, in character but are still taken up in the oneness of the whole."[1] 'Organic' is a way of capturing the unity and diversity inherent in creation.

For Bavinck, there are really only two worldviews: the theistic and the atheistic. We either believe in the one, true God (and all that entails) or we believe in something else. Regardless of whether we confess other gods or not, Bavinck calls that other worldview atheistic, because it does not trust in the Triune God. The closed, mechanical view is atheistic. A system where everything operates only by means of cause and effect cannot be compatible with Christian faith.[2] Bavinck wants to reject a mechanical view of the world, which he believes is inherently atheistic.

However, because the Christian worldview acknowledges the Triune God, this move away from mechanism takes a particular shape: organicism. Organicism, the principle that God created the world with both unity and diversity, is necessary for thinking about creation because the Creator of the universe is the Triune God. "The foundation for both diversity and unity is in God...Here is a unity that does not destroy but rather maintains diversity, and a diversity that does not come at the expense of unity, but rather unfolds it in its riches."[3]

According to James Eglinton, Bavinck has four guiding principles within his organic worldview:

First, "The created order is marked by simultaneous unity and diversity."[4] The world reflects the identity of God as three-in-one, though God is not "organic." "Reality therefore becomes somewhat triniform: life is a unity of different parts."[5] It is important that Bavinck is not looking out at the unity and diversity in the world and reading that back into God. He is not saying that God is a unity of different parts. Instead, he is saying that, because God has revealed himself as Triune, as three-in-one, we should expect his creation to reflect his character, however distantly. The direction is important. He is not "tinkering with the Trinity" because he is enamored with organicism, but instead is trying to think well about the creation because God is Triune. Eglinton makes this clear: "While he describes many things as 'organic', the notable exception to this pattern regards God himself. The deliberate intent of Bavinck's system, it seems, is to consistently describe the creation as organic and the Creator as Triune."[6]

At the core of Bavinck's explanation of the "organic worldview" is a theological concern that we take the Trinity seriously. If we interpret God as a monad (as merely "one" and not as Triune) we can tend to view the cosmos as exclusively mechanical.[7] Bavinck saw this in theologians who tried to reconcile the Christian faith to the mechanistic worldview of the day. They were left with the First Cause, or the Unmoved Mover, a clockmaker who created the world, wound it up, and let it go. Their accounts contained no traces of the living God of the Bible, the Triune God of grace. Whatever confessional documents they signed, Bavinck saw these systems as *functionally* denying the Trinity. For Bavinck, to begin one's worldview with God requires that one start with the Triune God revealed in Scripture. This starting point leads to an organic worldview that holds together both the unity and diversity of creation.

For Bavinck, one of the reasons we can speak of creation as organic, but cannot speak of God in the same way is the divine attribute of immutability. Divine immutability is the classically Christian way of saying that God does not change. "Every good gift and every perfect gift is from above, and comes down from the Father of lights, with whom there is no variation or shadow of turning" (James 1:17 NKJV). God does not change, but we do. God does not develop or improve. He is already perfect in himself. For us, change can be for better or worse. We can develop or deform when we change. God made us to grow from immaturity into maturity. We both *are* and *become*. We are organic, in that sense. God, however, does not become. He is perfect. Any change in God could never be growth or development or improvement. It would only be for the worse. In short, because God is already perfect, he has no need to change. There is nothing he needs to become, because he is already perfection. Creation develops and changes, but God is already perfect. Creation is organic, but God is not.

Bavinck's second guiding principle is that "unity precedes diversity."[8] While Bavinck believes that the organic worldview holds together both unity and diversity, he argues that unity comes first. He sees this in the creation account, where God first creates heaven and earth, then divides and fills it. The unity of creation comes first, then God distinguishes water from land, light from darkness. Then God fills the sea with various fish, the sky with various birds, and the lands with animals, each according to their kind. Bavinck seeks to preserve the orderliness of creation. It is not a work of chaos or confusion — God created all things according to his purpose and set them in their place in his creation.

Bavinck not only speaks of creation as a whole as 'organic,' but also speaks this way of the church. Here, too, unity precedes diversity. Though God saves and elects individuals, the church "is an organism, not an aggregate; the whole, in its case, precedes the parts." The church is not simply the collection of individuals, but the body of Christ who gains its life from its head, Jesus Christ.[9] In the church, as in creation, the whole precedes the parts.[10]

Third, "The organism's shared life is orchestrated by a common idea"[11] This organic creation is not disorderly. The world may appear to be an endless mass of events or particles, which come and go like waves on the ocean. However, if we look more deeply, Bavinck argues, we will discover "a harmony and fitness for purpose in the multiplicity."[12] The world cannot be an accident. Just like bodily organs have different tasks, yet work together to run the body, so too with creation. Unity in diversity means that the distinct facets of creation complement, rather than compete with each other.[13]

Fourth, "The organism has a drive toward its goal"[14] — the glory of the Triune God. Again, God is not organic, God is triune. However, God is glorified as creation maintains its unity and diversity, as it moves towards its end in the new heavens and the new earth. An organic worldview faithfully considers the purpose of creation. Bavinck critiques Darwin both for his mechanical view, but also for lacking a proper "end" for life. Creation and life have a purpose. They do not exist for their own sake, but for the sake of glorifying God. The first question of the Westminster Shorter Catechism echoes this organic position: "What is the chief end of man? Man's chief end is to glorify God and to enjoy him forever."[15] Organicism stands against mechanism, which treats people and creation as a set of machine parts with no discernible purpose, and against dynamism, which views life as a force or energy. Only organicism can properly account for the unity, diversity, and purpose of creation.

Just as Christians held a "worldview" long before the word was commonly used to describe it, Christians have held to an organic understanding of creation even if they never used the word. The world was created by the Triune God to be a place united by his wisdom and purpose, with one goal (the glory of God), but also with immense and beautiful diversity. While Bavinck's formulation responds to the specific questions of his day (and overlaps with our own), this basic position has been shared by Christians throughout the ages.

FORMED ACCORDING TO GOD'S WISDOM

Bavinck's organicism — and the Christian worldview more generally — is not the product first of philosophical speculation, but biblical reflection. Organic "unity in diversity" is not the best option simply because the other options fall apart, but because it is the way things actually are. "It does not approach nature with a theory but rather takes it as it gives itself to us"[16] Behind the language of mechanism, dynamism, and organicism is the reality spoken of in Romans 11:33-36:

> "Oh, the depth of the riches of the wisdom and
> knowledge of God!
>   How unsearchable his judgments,
>   and his paths beyond tracing out!
> "Who has known the mind of the Lord?
>   Or who has been his counselor?"
> "Who has ever given to God,
>   that God should repay them?"
> For from him and through him and for him are all
> things.
>   To him be the glory forever! Amen."

Out of the depths of God's wisdom, he made the world and everything in it. The world is not a haphazard jumble of atoms, because it has its source in the wisdom of God. God is the source, means, and goal of creation.

First, God is the source of creation. "From him...are all things." God made the world according to his wisdom. The world is organized by certain ideas. Things not only exist, but exist in a certain way, according to a certain pattern. "They [the ideas] are to be considered objective ideas, which give order and coherence to the multiplicity of parts and bind them in an organic unity. They make things into what each is in its own particularity. Just as an artist lays down his idea in the marble, so God realizes his word in the world. Herein, however, lies this great distinction. Humans can make only works of art or instruments, which are always transcended — more or less — by the idea. God, however, creates beings which, while remaining instruments in his hands (Is 10:15), nonetheless absorb the idea and realize themselves through spontaneous activity."[17] We *make* things, but God *creates*. The ideas of the good, the true, and the beautiful always stand above our works and form the standard that judges them. God's wisdom *is* the standard. God does not obey any standards outside of himself. However, God has made creation so that it unfolds his wisdom. God not only gives life to plants, but makes them able to bear seeds and produce more according to their own kind. He does the same with fish, birds, and animals. He makes things what they are and, by his wisdom, they can become, move, and develop toward what God made them to become. As Al Wolters says, "As God the craftsman fashions the world, Wisdom is the standard by which he works."[18]

There is an energy, a force that moves and directs the world (the dynamists are right on this point). God is not only the source of all creation (the "push" that got things going), but he is also the goal of all creation ("pulling" all things toward his purpose). For "to him are all things." "Divine energy is the source of all powers and energies in the creatures, and because this divine energy is not blind but is rather led by divine wisdom, the powers and workings in the natural world also demonstrate direction and course."[19] This distinction between blind forces and divine wisdom is a crucial difference between organicism and dynamism (of the old or contemporary variety). Things do change, there is movement, and there are forces at work in the universe. However, it is the Triune God who works to guide creation according to his wisdom and purpose. For "through him are all things." God is the source, goal, and means of creation. He upholds, guides, and directs creation as it develops, according to his wisdom, to the end that all creation would glorify God. This is the Christian confession on the basis of Scripture, which is being expressed through the language of "organic."

This confession that "from him and through him and to him are all things" — far from leading to a rejection of science and scientific discovery — leads Christians to be at the forefront of science. Because we believe in both the stability and the development of the world around us, we can study — in a disciplined way — the natural laws and changes in the world. Because, as Christians, we believe there are genuine ideas of goodness, truth, and beauty, we can actively pursue the ideas being worked out in all the corners of creation. Because, as Christians, we believe in both the unity and diversity of creation, we believe ideas, ideals, and categories are real because they exist in the mind of God. We also believe that the world changes and develops toward God's intended purpose for creation. We do not need to deny any of the truths of materialism or dynamism, but we can rightly hold them together.

Bavinck makes this argument using the language of Platonism and Darwinism. We look out at the world and see unity and diversity, stability and change. We need to deny none of them, for the Christian worldview takes reality as it is — created by the Living God:

> "The typical, the general, the sort remains; one does not [gather] grapes from thorns or figs from thistles; a plant does not become an animal and an animal a human or a human an angel. This...is the truth of Platonism. And yet we also see the whole world, with all that it contains, in constant movement;

there is an unbroken emergence and departure, a restlessly born becoming and dying; no creature is like another, or even fully like itself, for two moments. The only thing permanent here below is impermanence. That is the truth of Darwinism...These are the facts that stand firm for everyone. To deny them or to sacrifice one series of them for another is of no benefit."[20]

In the rise of modern science, there are two important facets to remember: "(1) It was precisely *Christians* who were exhibiting a new interest in creation/nature *for theological reasons*; and (2) this interest was clearly not mutually exclusive with belief in God and an affirmation of transcendence."[21] The Christian faith drives and makes possible a commitment to scientific discovery and knowledge, even as it resists the takeover of materialism. Unity and diversity, stability and change, are part of the same whole creation because God formed it according to his wisdom and guides it toward his purposes.

CHANGE OR DEVELOPMENT?

One of the hallmarks of Darwinian evolution is the notion that species adapt and change. There is development from primitive single cell organisms to aquatic animals to amphibians to reptiles to birds and mammals. However, despite appearances, a mechanistic Darwinian understanding of the world cannot account for actual "development." What was lost in Darwin was what Bavinck saw as key to an organic (and, therefore, Christian) standpoint: we forgot what things were for. "In the mechanical view, there is no place for development in the actual sense." All differences are accidental, not development or progress. "Nothing *becomes*, because there is nothing that *needs* to become, that *must* become. There is no goal and no starting point — and development is based precisely on both of these things. It describes the path that leads from one to the other. It is possible only when things are something, when they have a "nature," a *principium* and *radix* of all their attributes and activities, and when they, by virtue of that nature, must then become something and have to meet a destination. There is thus no development in machines and instruments. It is only found in organic beings."[22]

The difference between change and development is purpose. Mechanism (and Darwinism as a form of that) can account for change. It can describe how molecules move or theorize about how birds' beaks developed relative to the food they ate. "Survival" becomes the only purpose of any living being in the world. Life — the life of the individual, the life of the species, life on this planet — becomes an end in and of itself. But what is life actually for? What is humanity and what is it meant for? Why are we here? These are the questions of development that mechanism cannot answer. It may have some skill in explaining how we got here, but it cannot tell us where to go from here. Development requires purpose. As James K. A. Smith says, it requires a cause that pulls us, not just pushes us. He says this about the shifts in the modern world:

> "Part of the fallout of such a metaphysical shift is the loss of final causality (a cause that attracts or "pulls"), eclipsing any teleology for things/nature. Understanding something is no longer a matter of understanding its "essence" and hence its telos (end). Instead we get the "mechanistic" universe that we still inhabit today, in which *efficient* causality (a cause that "pushes") is the only causality and can only be discerned by empirical observation."[23]

Mechanism only allows for causes that push. A causes B, B causes C, and C causes D. What it has lost — and what must be recovered in a Christian worldview — is a cause that pulls. A moves toward B, B is drawn to C, C is meant to become D. The Christian worldview holds that there are not only causes that stand behind us and move us forward, but also causes/purposes/ends that stand in front of creation and draw us forward as well. There is development because creation has a purpose, including us. This is why we not only change, but can become and grow. Not only do all things come from God and through God's creative word, but all things are *to him*. That is, he is the end and goal of our life and the life of all creation. As Bavinck says, "[T]he Christian worldview gives us the right to speak of a development in all things and pertaining to the entire world, because here is a divine thought that must be realized in the passing of time. God has created all things for his own will. He makes all things subservient to the honor of his name. From him and through him and to him are all things."[24]

INHABITING A CHRISTIAN VIEW OF THE WORLD

How can we grow to see the world organically? Our contemporary culture fractures unity and diversity, stability and change —it has lost the ability to consider what things are for. The dominant ways of seeing the world are mechanistic or dynamic, as we have explored in this and the previous chapter. Even if we are convinced that "from him and through him and to him are all things" and that God created the world according to his wisdom and guides it toward the end of glorifying his name, how can we be shaped to actually see the world this way — to see it as it actually is? Is it enough simply to read this chapter and make sure we have the right ideas about mechanism, dynamism, and organicism in our heads?

No.

As important as thinking clearly is (and I would not have written a whole book working through Christian worldview if I wasn't convinced of that), we cannot inhabit a Christian worldview simply by thinking the right thoughts or banishing the wrong ideas. Worship is one of the key places where we form our vision of the world. Robust Christian worship can be a place where the fractures of the modern world are mended, where we can see anew the world as it truly is. As James K. A. Smith says, "In short, the practice of Christian worship resists two sorts of reductionism: a dualistic, supernaturalistic gnosticism, on the one hand, and a materialistic, flattened naturalism, on the other."[25]

In worship, we not only confess, but learn that "from him and through him and to him are all things." Just as the story of Scripture stretches from creation to new creation and moves through the story of sin and redemption, so does our worship service. When we come in worship and praise, we honor the purpose for which we were made — life before the face of God. We come and acknowledge — not just with words, but in song and action — that our life comes from God. For the Lord has given us life and being and preserved us by his providence. As Alan Noble says, "Your existence is good and right and significant because a loving God intentionally created you and continues to give you your every breath."[26] All the moments of thanksgiving in worship attest to this wonderful truth. It is not only affirmed, but internalized through worship.

In confession and in corporate prayer, we practice viewing what Al Wolters calls the structure and direction of creation. Structure refers to the substances, essence, or nature of a thing. We acknowledge the goodness of creation and the goodness of our Creator. What he has made is good. However, we also confess that, at our lead and as a result of the sin of our first parents, creation has moved away from the direction God has set for it. We confess not only our personal sins and failings, but the fallenness of creation, which groans for redemption. We confess, as Wolters says, "The distortion or perversion of creation through the fall on the one hand and the redemption and restoration of creation in Christ on the other."[27]

In baptism, we experience the waters of creation, the waters of judgment at the flood, the rescue through the Red Sea, the washing of cleansing, and the new birth of the kingdom of God. In baptism, we are called back into the story of redemption, recalled to trust in the cleansing and claiming work of Christ. But in baptism, we are also pulled forward into a life in Christ, a life of repentance, a life as one who has been sealed as Christ's own forever in the waters of baptism. The end and purpose of our life is seen in the baptismal waters.

In the Lord's Supper, the push and pull of our life are brought together in the bread and the cup. We remember the perfect sacrifice offered once on the cross by our Lord Jesus Christ for the sin of the world. The redemption of God in Christ stands behind us and pushes us forward into union with and imitation of Christ. We are who we are because of what he has done for us. We know the Father because Jesus has made Him known to us. His work stands behind us and propels us forward, which is tasted and enacted at the table. At the table, we also have a foretaste of the coming kingdom of God. We eat the bread and drink the cup in anticipation of the day when Christ will come and set all things right and make all things new. On that day, there will be a great banquet table and Jesus Christ himself will sit at the head with all the saints of all the ages. At the table, we get a taste of the future, a promised future that pulls us forward and enlivens our activity and imagination as we wait. Between the push of the cross and the pull of the kingdom is the communion we have with Christ at the table. In the supper itself, the fractures of our modern world are mended as we eat and drink in joyful remembrance, communion, and hope.

In the offering of our gifts, we acknowledge that all we have comes as a gift from God. In the benediction and sending, we are renewed in our purpose in the world. For Christians today to recover this Christian worldview, to see reality as it is and not the distorted slices modernity presents to us, we need more than lectures, courses, and books. We need a renewal of Christian worship.

CONCLUSION

"From him and through him and to him are all things." In order to understand creation well, we do not need to deny the insights of either dynamism or mechanism. They are, however, the two main options that arise when we begin by rejecting the Triune God of Scripture. In the last chapter, we explored the deficiencies of these two positions. In this chapter, we made the positive case for the organic worldview as the way to hold together what modernity has sought to rip apart. God created the world. He is the source of all things. He created it by his Word and according to his Wisdom. He created it for a purpose — that it might glorify him. This "organicism" holds together the unity and diversity, stability and changeability of creation. The Christian worldview is a better foundation for science than mechanism and a better account of transcendence than dynamism.

The way to recover this Christian view of the world — taking world as it truly is, the creation of the Triune God — is through worship. Logical arguments have their place, but it is as we sing and pray, as we are washed and eat and drink, that we will have our eyes opened to see anew both the creation and the Creator.

CHAPTER 6
NO FOUNDATION
MORALITY IN THE MODERN WORLD

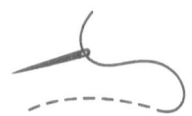

"You will not die; for God knows that when you eat of it your eyes will be opened, and you will be like God, knowing good and evil."
- Genesis 3:4-5

"This contemporary social imaginary is crystallized in terms of authenticity. So the primary — yea, only — value in such a world is choice."
- Alan Noble

"We could be like God." As Eve stared at the fruit on the forbidden tree, these words must have echoed in her mind. "If we reach out and grab the fruit, if we take and eat it, then *we* can take the place of God. We will no longer need to look to God to know good and evil, for we will know it for ourselves. We can step forward and take the reins of history for ourselves. We can make the way for ourselves." Eve reached out, took the fruit, ate it, and gave some to her husband and the world was never the same.

What is presented to Eve as a *temptation* is, in the modern world, a *model* for living a true moral life. We believe that we must set aside the oppressive rules of religion and society and brave the wind and waves of the world with our hands on the tiller. Never mind looking for true North — we must each find our own moral compass.

What modernity calls "courage," though, Christianity has called the "curse." The seduction of the snake was not an invitation to freedom, but to bondage for our first parents and for all of creation. In a similar way, the modern world has worked to forge a morality apart from God, where humans can take the center stage of history. Yet, this 'freedom' has only led to fracture.

In this chapter, we will look at the two main shifts in the modern world with regard to morality. Our culture has changed from the family to the individual as the primary moral unit. We have also shifted from God to humans as the source of moral law and authority. We will also explore how, as a result, the moral order has fractured in multiple directions. These shifts have caused us either to abandon moral responsibility with determinism or to be crushed under the full weight of constructing our own morality with relativism. We will end the chapter by considering how recovering God as the divine lawgiver holds together what modernity has sought to rip apart.

THE RISE OF THE INDIVIDUAL

In the previous chapters, we have talked extensively about the fractures that have opened up in the modern world. The unified understanding of human knowledge has come apart at the seams, as we often feel forced to make a false choice between mind and body, sensation and thinking, rationalism and empiricism. The Christian worldview knits back together where our understanding of the world has started to fray. The unified understanding of change and nature has also been put under pressure, as materialism has dominated our public consciousness, even as dynamism overcorrects in the opposite direction. However much we might understand and see these fractures in our world, for most of us, we feel the fracture of the modern world most deeply in the realm of morality. It is not in the physical world, but the moral world where the deepest fissures have opened.

As with knowledge and nature, the fractures in the moral world have moved in two different directions, both of which contain some truth, but both of which deny other essential truths. Behind these shifts in morality, however, is a more fundamental shift: the rise of the individual as the principal unit of morality.

The modern world, particularly after the Enlightenment, was built on the principle of personal autonomy. In his famous essay, "What is Enlightenment," Immanuel Kant defended the motto of the Enlightenment project, "Dare to know."

> "Have the courage to use your own understanding," is therefore the motto of the enlightenment. Laziness and cowardice are the reasons why such a large part of mankind gladly remain minors all their lives, long after nature has freed them from external guidance. They are the reasons why it is so easy for others to set themselves up as guardians. It is so comfortable to be a minor. If I have a book that thinks for me, a pastor who acts as my conscience, a physician who prescribes my diet, and so on — then I have no need to exert myself. I have no need to think, if only I can pay; others will take care of that disagreeable business for me.[1]

Kant champions thinking for oneself. It is a sign of immaturity to take things simply on authority and let others do our thinking for us. Instead, we need the courage to think for ourselves and break the shackles of authority over us (including, specifically, the authority of the church and doctrine). This concept of Enlightenment requires a certain notion of freedom to make sense. Kant continues,

> This enlightenment requires nothing but *freedom* — and the most innocent of all that may be called "freedom": freedom to make public use of one's reason in all matters. Now I hear the cry from all sides: "Do not argue!" The officer says: "Do not argue — drill!" The tax collector: "Do not argue — pay!" The pastor: "Do not argue — believe!" Only one ruler in the world says: "Argue as much as you please, but obey!" We find restrictions on freedom everywhere. But which restriction is harmful to enlightenment? Which restriction is innocent, and which advances enlightenment? I reply: the public use of one's reason must be free at all times, and this alone can bring enlightenment to mankind.[2]

We have all been shaped by this concept of Enlightenment and even enriched in many ways. Kant's charge that the church encourages obedience and never allows for disagreements may be true in isolated contexts, but does not hold true historically or in contemporary life. However, notice what Kant doesn't even have to say. Who is this freedom for? Who is to be enlightened? The individual. We, as individuals, are called to rule ourselves, to think for ourselves, to be enlightened.

Kant's call to "think for ourselves" only makes sense because a prior, unspoken shift has already been made — the individual has replaced the family as the fundamental moral unit. In the Bible, individuals have dignity and agency. They have moral responsibility and the power to exercise their will. The Christian worldview does not deny individuality or the role and importance of individual people. However, the fundamental unit of life and society in the Bible is the family. At creation, God places Adam and Eve together into a family. The drama of the patriarchs is a family drama. It involves the quest for children. Abraham and Sarah, Isaac and Rebekah, Jacob and Rachel and Leah are individuals, but are never considered simply as autonomous individuals. They are imbedded into the context of families and their decisions are weighed not only by their impact on themselves, but on their families, their future, and the whole family's faithfulness to God. Israel as a nation was a family of tribes. Their relationship as a people was that of a family writ large. The nation was one huge family, built out of smaller families. Even when family breaks down or is absent or is dysfunctional in some ways, it is still the family that is the fundamental unit of society. When God speaks of how we are saved, it is not simply as individuals, but through adoption into the family of God. No person is ever considered as an entity unto themselves, but we are always already embedded into covenantal relationship with family and community.

Contrast this picture with that inherited in our contemporary culture from Kant and others. Even if Kant would have envisioned his Enlightenment as benevolent and not selfish, it has had a profound impact on how our contemporary society views the individual's relationship to everyone else. Instead of covenantal bonds and moral relationships being part of the fabric of human life, they are viewed as incidental to life. A family is not a given, but a choice. It is a convenient way of structuring our personal lives for the mutual benefit of the individual. However, it is the individual who is always to be considered. A family is a set of individuals, instead of individuals being a subset of a family.

When people bemoan that we live in an "individualistic society," they are often complaining about the self-centeredness prevalent in our world. However, selfishness and self-centeredness are not exclusive to the modern West. Luther, at the beginning of the reformation, but with his feet still firmly in the medieval world, described sinful humanity as *homo incurvatus in se* — a human being turned in upon himself. Selfishness manifests throughout the stories of the Old and New Testaments, which were far from the individualism of our day. Even in cultures that consider the family unit to be central, this in itself does not curb selfishness or the wicked behavior that can stem from it.

What is different is that our culture views the individual as the fundamental moral and ethical unit. As such, the good of the individual takes precedence over the good of the family. Such a transition has had many benefits. The "good of the family" or the "good of the community" cannot be used to excuse the abuse of individuals or injustice against groups of people. The rise of the individual has enabled many people to move out of unhealthy situations and move into situations where their talents can flourish. We should not underestimate this or pine for a golden age of "family values." However, we need to recognize that there has also been incredible loss with the shift to individualism. Just as in knowledge the modern world sought to break everything down into its smallest parts (ideas and sensations), and in the natural world it too sought to break everything into atoms, elements, and molecules, so in the moral world, the society and family have been broken down into the smallest parts — the individual.[3]

Individualism hurts children, hurts marriages, and hurts those who are single, or widowed. Individualism hurts children when it infects their parents. While some parents sacrifice themselves for the sake of the broader family, the trend is alarmingly in the opposite direction. Children can be seen as an inconvenience when our primary moral responsibility is to ourselves and our fulfillment. Only secondarily and incidentally are we responsible for those entrusted to us. Individualism also hurts children when it infects them and makes it difficult for them to consider their actions in light of the larger family or community. Young children might naturally see themselves as at the center of the universe, but our culture and technology only reinforce this view, they do not challenge it. Much of what is considered "heroic" behavior in our modern families is, in fact, individualistic and selfish. Many of the leaders and gurus from the business and sports world — who we are taught to admire — frequently and habitually sacrificed their family for their dreams. Eighty-hour work weeks might move your business to six figures within two years, but what about the people you leave at home to be at the office. People will leave spouses and children in order to follow their passion or live their truth.

In a similar way, individualism can hurt marriage. Selfishness in marriage will always lead to pain and difficulty, but when marriage is not viewed as a man and woman becoming one flesh, entering into a covenantal relationship, but merely a contract between two individuals for mutual benefit, then this selfishness becomes enshrined into marriage itself.

Individualism also says to the single or widowed that we are all fundamentally alone in the world. Instead of enfolding them into a new family or new community, individualism calls for them to care for themselves and make their own choices, be courageous enough to think and care for themselves. "Dare to know" quickly morphs into dare to be alone.

On a moral register, individualism is deeply related to autonomy. Autonomy is a word that means we make our own rules, we are "self-ruled." It denies an external moral order and calls on each person to form his or her own morality, to form his or her own moral world, because no such morality actually exists. This denial of an external moral world and of God as the lawgiver has led to many of the moral fractures of our age.

FRACTURE 1: DETERMINISM

The denial of God, coupled with the shift from the family to the individual as the primary moral unit, has led to the moral life tearing in two directions. First, alongside the rise of mechanism in science, we have the rise of determinism with regard to the human will. Determinism claims that, just as everything in the physical world is the result of cause and effect, the same is true when it comes to human actions. There is no genuine free will. What we believe to be free will is an illusion, the product of a thousand unknown and complex causes that work upon us so that we make the "choices" we make. There is an unbroken chain of events that led to this moment and an unbroken chain that will lead forward from it. Each link is forged not by a choice or act of will, but by a natural consequence of natural forces. For determinism, it is not enough to say we are *influenced* by our background, our circumstances, or even our current emotional state — instead, these factors *determine* our actions.

However, this account does not match the world as we find it. In the world we inhabit, we are faced with choices. We do have the power of will. We can choose not to help our sister when she falls down, even if we know we should. We can feel the pull to self-preservation when running from a bear, but turn back to grab a stranger's hand to pull them up so that they can run as well.

As Bavinck points out, our free will is something we cannot avoid. "Where in reality we are free, we are in any case unable to find freedom to not be free. The reality, the possibility even, of freedom is contestable, but the right and duty toward freedom is indisputable."[4] We might find ourselves with less choice or less power to choose or exercise our will, but the "right and duty" remains. We are not free to be completely passive in this world and go along with the flow of life. There are causes and influences upon our lives, but we have the power, duty, and responsibility to act not simply according to nature, but according to character. "This phenomenon is strikingly majestic. Everywhere in the world, strict causality prevails; nothing occurs by chance; everything has a cause. But in the moral order of the world, a power appears before us that seems to take no account of this causality."[5] The human will is influenced, but not bound, by causes or nature.

Whether or not determinism has its own inherent problems, it is important to realize that no one actually lives as if our world is deterministic. Consider the most strident determinist, someone who denies free will and believes all our actions are solely the result of stimuli or influences. This person still undoubtably works to change their circumstances, is active in their world, and even attempts to convince their neighbor of the truth of their determinism. They might argue that we do not have a will or genuine agency, but they constantly exercise their own agency and demonstrate their will as they do so.

It is rare to find someone who holds strictly to determinism, but its influence permeates our cultural moment. For the sake of giving it a label, we will call this "soft determinism." One of the consequences of soft determinism is the denial of moral responsibility and the rise of victimhood. There are no moral actions, simply actions. Moral categories of right and wrong, good and evil (which require an outside objective standard) are done away with in favor of more personal and therapeutic categories. We see this most clearly when talking, not about what is good, but what has gone wrong. As James K. A. Smith notes, moral issues have moved from being considered as "sin" to "sickness." "What's wrong with me is more like a disease that befalls me than a disorder for which I am responsible."[6] If what is wrong with the human condition is ultimately like an illness — whether social or mental or physical — then it is not really my fault. Sure, I can try to live cleanly and safely. I can do my best to avoid high risk behaviors, but when I get an illness, I am a victim, not a responsible agent. An illness is something that happens *to me*. It must be treated. We employ techniques to alleviate symptoms or deal with the disease, but human persons (or society itself) become patients to be treated, not sinners in need of repentance and conversion. When we move from saying people are influenced by their environments to saying they are *products* of their environment, we avoid moral responsibility for our actions. "The moral is transferred to a therapeutic register; in doing so we move from responsibility to victimhood."[7]

There are two difficulties in challenging this therapeutic turn in our cultural understanding of sin and morality. First, it is so pervasive it is difficult to see. It is the water in which we swim. The language of wellness, wholeness, healing, anxiety, satisfaction, self-actualization, contentment, symptoms, sickness, self-care and more is such a part of everyday speech — the language that expresses our worldview — that we barely notice it anymore. Second, there is danger in denying the truth contained in therapeutic language and techniques. Concern about the rise of "victimhood" as a moral category is not to deny the reality of victims. Some people's willful actions create incredible damage to others. Sometimes our wounds and scars are not the result of any direct choice on our part, but the choice of another to harm us. We need to be able to acknowledge, recognize, and even fight for victims, without treating victimhood as fundamental for all social and personal ills.

Concern that our culture treats every problem as an illness or syndrome is also not to deny the reality of mental and physical illness. Mental health problems are real. Christians believe that God can miraculously heal our bodies apart from any medical intervention or work from doctors, but also that God usually works his healing through the means of doctors and medicine and the healing processes God has created our bodies to have. While we also believe that God can miraculously heal our mental illnesses or anxiety or depression apart from the work of any counselor or psychologist, we believe that God usually works his healing through the means of those who have honed their gifts to aid in healing our minds.

To be concerned about the eclipse of moral responsibility is also not to deny the power of society and community as it shapes our lives. We are influenced by culture, or else we would not take the time to write a book exploring culture and worldview. We are influenced by our past, our context, our ideas, and our community in deep and profound ways.

However, soft determinism moves the therapeutic language beyond where it belongs to encompass all of life. As we saw with mechanism in chapter 4, soft determinism takes the good of therapeutic and medical interventions and looks at the entire world exclusively through that lens. It is the hammer that looks at all of human life like a nail. In doing so, we attempt to set aside the moral responsibility to act with character and consider our actions and choices in light of the good, the true, and the beautiful.

Determinism — whether hard or soft — frays our world because it denies the existence of a moral world. By appealing to cause and effect, or reducing our problems to a matter of sickness instead of sin, it is part of the blame-shifting human impulse that goes all the way back to the Garden of Eden. God told Adam that, of all the trees in the Garden, there was one in the center that he must not eat, the tree of the knowledge of good and evil. One day Eve, Adam's wife, encountered a snake in the garden. The snake tempted but did not coerce Eve to eat the fruit. He sowed mistrust and questioned God's good intentions for Adam and Eve. Eve trusted and listened to the serpent over the commands of God. When God confronted our first parents, they blamed others instead of taking responsibility for their own moral decisions. Adam blamed Eve. "The woman you put here with me—she gave me some fruit from the tree, and I ate it." (Gen 3:12) Eve blamed the serpent. "The serpent tricked me, and I ate." (3:13) We can almost hear, implicit in their responses, "It wasn't my fault."

Al Wolters rightly reminds us that this impulse did not die with Adam and Eve, "Deeply ingrained in the children of Adam is the tendency to blame some aspect of creation (and by implication the Creator) rather than their own rebellion for the misery of their condition."[8] Someone or something else is responsible for their decisions. Their actions are not "sinful," but merely symptoms of sickness. If the sickness was treated, then they would be okay, but right now, they cannot help the way they acted. "The great danger is always to single out some aspect or phenomenon of God's good creation and identify it, rather than the alien intrusion or human apostasy, as the villain in the drama of human life."[9]

By denying God and denying our human responsibility as moral agents, determinism misreads the world. It misdiagnoses the fundamental moral problem of human life not as sin, but as sickness, and therefore suggests the wrong treatment. Ibuprofen is good when you have a headache, but it cannot fix a broken leg. You can take more and more (even stronger and more addictive pain relievers), but the pills will not set your leg, or even perform the surgery you need. Just as a misdiagnosis is deadly for our bodies, it is even more so for our souls.

FRACTURE 2: RELATIVISM

If the fracture of determinism is to deny that there is a moral world at all, the fracture of relativism is to say that the moral world is simply a product of history and community. There is no absolute and unchanging moral law, but only the standards of a given community at a given period of time. Morality develops and evolves as history moves forward. When it comes to morality, there is no absolute truth, only *my* truth or *our* truth. Today's truth may not be truth tomorrow.

Moral relativism begins by paying attention to history. Human cultures have changed over time and differ across ages, countries, and continents. Some behaviors or actions perfectly normal in the third century BC would now be abhorrent to people in twenty-first century North America. Some of what makes perfect sense in sub-Saharan Africa would seem illogical in South Korea. And in diverse communities, we may not have to go farther than a few houses down the street to encounter very different moral sensibilities and convictions. The realization that society and people's sense of morality changes over time is not new. What is new in the modern world is that God as the divine source of morality is removed or at least bracketed out of the equation. Then, these differences of morality are treated not as moral questions, but as historical ones.

In short, history studies what 'is' and what 'was,' but not what 'ought to be.' Ethics and morality are the realm of 'should' and 'ought.' Morality does not describe what people actually do, but what they should do (even though they often don't). The study of history is a good discipline. Even in the realm of morality, this historical turn was initially helpful. It can be illuminating to see how people actually behaved and how moral life and moral arguments have developed. However, when this method is applied limitlessly, there is great loss. Studying how people have behaved will never, in itself, get us to how people should live. Moreover, simply naming the various ways that people's behavior and understanding have changed over time tends to treat morality as an evolutionary process, leaving no place for the absolute. Historical and psychological research won't be enough to discover morality. As Bavinck says, "The hope, however, is vain that one shall obtain an ethic if one analyzes human tendencies and actions precisely, or that one shall find the true religion through the practice of religious psychology and the history of religions, or that one could organize a society as long as the social instincts were first studied with precision."[10] Just because something is the way it is, does not mean it is how it is supposed to be.

For the proponents of moral relativism, our current beliefs about right and wrong, about the true, the good, and the beautiful, do not reflect timeless truths, but instead constitute very historical and contingent realities. Morality, therefore, is not rooted in an absolute good or an absolute law about what we should do, but what our community or culture approves or disapproves. Or, in our current moment, what we *personally* approve or disapprove. What we believe about abortion, marriage, poverty, sickness, or criminal justice is not based on some objective standard, but our social location as 21st century North Americans who are part of a particular community, with a certain form of education and background. Moral relativism views truth as relative to our time and place or even relative to the individual who holds it.

Relativism shares with Kant the firm belief in autonomy. Humans rule themselves. There is no divine lawgiver, so humans must dare to search for themselves. However, whereas Kant, in rejecting God as the lawgiver, sought with all his might to form a new, firm, and absolute foundation for morality, relativism believes there is no absolute foundation. Humans make their own laws about good and evil, right and wrong, and they do so in history and in community. "Relativism appears, then, to be impartial, as it wants to know of no fixed norms and claims to be concerned with and to speak of only the concrete, the historical. But it makes the relative itself into the absolute and therefore exchanges true freedom for coercion, real faith for superstition."[11]

The modern project ends with either a flight from history and being trapped by history. We can try to smooth out all the rough edges of moral history and the diversity of beliefs in order to find the most basic shared convictions of all humanity on morality and seek to build a new moral system from there. The number of attempts at this project — all with different conclusions — points to its futility. The other option is to reduce morality to history and community. While the rise of moral relativism is often connected with what has been dubbed 'postmodernity,' it has its roots in the modernity's concern for history.

However, this position has deep and troubling consequences. First, if morality is determined by the individual or community, there is no basis for saying anything another community does is wrong. James K. A. Smith hits the nail on the head, "If our moral categories are nothing more than the expressions of some community's preferences, then there will be no recourse to critique a *bad* community's bad morals."[12] Each community is 'living its truth,' which cannot be assailed or critiqued from the outside. There is no shared standard by which we can judge, for each community determines the standard for themselves.

Second, while forming our own standards for morality appears like freedom, it is actually a burden. Our world prizes a certain version of authenticity and being "true to yourself." We need to discover our true self — not the self imposed by outside voices or forces or rules — and live according to who we *really* are. However, authenticity cuts both ways. As Alan Noble notes, "this is both exciting and frightening. It means we don't have to follow in our parent's footsteps. We don't have to adopt our community's values or its vision of the good life. We are free to discover the meaning of our own life — but we're also burdened to discover it."[13] We cannot accept the meaning given to us by our family or community. We *must* discover it for ourselves. And every time we think that we have reached the bottom and core of ourselves and shed all outside influences and found our true self, we are left alone in wondering if we truly reached the core or if there are more layers to peel back. "To be "true to myself" is to be "true" in an unconventional way. To be true to yourself is categorically different from being true in an empirical or logical sense, because there is no external or objective way to judge or reassure ourselves. How can you ever be sure that you are being true to yourself? How can you even know if you are being authentic? You are utterly alone in your judgment — sovereign, but alone. And to make matters worse, you cannot trust yourself. The human mind is capable of tremendous self-deception. Maybe you are least true to yourself when you are trying to be true to yourself!"[14]

The modern project is an attempt to create a new foundation for life apart from God. It seeks to hold together knowledge, the world, and morality apart from the one who created them all. Life apart from God contains a rejection of any authority above and beyond human life. "In the modern world, meaning cannot be imposed upon us from an outside source."[15] Not religion, not government, not society, not anything can make meaning for us, or stand in judgment over us. We must stand in judgment ourselves and stand in judgment over ourselves. Ultimately, we travel this road alone. "Everyone is on their own private journey of self-discovery and self-expression, so that at times, modern life feels like billions of people in the same room shouting their own name so that everyone else knows they exist and who they are — which is a fairly accurate description of social media."[16] What a heavy burden to carry, especially if we carry it alone.

Third, we are made to live in a coherent moral order. When the moral order is cut down, people will start looking for something greater than themselves to ground their actions. Even over a hundred years ago, Bavinck could already see where the death of objective morality would lead. "Because a person always needs some form of stability, however, the grave and in no sense imaginary danger quickly arises that through this one-sided historical viewpoint, he is led to a counterfeit nationalism, to a narrow chauvinism, to a fanaticism about race and instinct."[17] Bavinck had already seen in his lifetime the rise of Aryanism and its rejection of the Jewishness of Jesus. He saw that the vacuum opened up by the breaking of the moral order would soon be filled by people who claimed moral authority and certitude. He saw eugenics and theories of racial origins, traits, and superiority taking hold throughout Europe. He died before this counterfeit nationalism, narrow chauvinism, and fanaticism about race could bear some of its most bitter fruit, but the 20th century was littered with its casualties. Even today, the rise of online radicalization reminds us that those who project moral certainty and foster community will find a ready following, no matter what that moral system contains.

It would seem that moral relativism would lead to anarchy. Without any objective standards and without the ability to critique anyone else, we would expect a free-for-all of vice and wickedness. While relativism had led to moral chaos, it has not — at this point — led to complete societal chaos. Why not?

According to Alan Noble, there are two main reasons we have not dissolved into anarchy as a society. First, our current culture has defaulted not to a ruthless selfishness, but a "do no harm" selfishness. "Do no harm" selfishness suggests that I can do whatever I want (and live by whatever moral code suits me best) as long as it does not actively harm you. I will live my truth and you live yours, as long as no one gets hurt. Alan Noble notes, "With the loss of a moral order established through religion, modern people are left with "human concerns" and gravitate toward universal benevolence."[18] Like all other modern values, it is optional, but most people opt into it. One of the few shared values left among the majority of people in the West is that we should not actively work to harm one another. This curbs some of society's more destructive tendencies. However, it is only an optional value in the modern world, so if increasingly people refuse to play by the rules of "do no harm," moral chaos will spill over into societal breakdown.

Second, most people are pragmatic. Being kind usually works to make life enjoyable, while being a jerk does not. Noble again, "Even when you give people freedom to determine morality for themselves, they generally choose to live peaceful, orderly lives...On the whole, being evil is a terrible way to live, and a pragmatical humanism is beneficial."[19] However, again, there is no firm basis for this conviction, so if circumstances change (i.e., being a bully actually helps you get ahead in life), we could see more significant breakdown.

Basically, the reason that moral relativism has not led to anarchy is that our culture is still living off the borrowed capital of Christianity. Though the modern project has sought a morality independent of God (and thus led to the breakdown we have seen in our moral world today), the full consequences have not yet been felt because our current cultural mores are still (despite appearances) shaped in significant ways by the Christian faith. Once that influence is eclipsed, all bets are off.

THE DIVINE LAWGIVER

Two shifts took place in the modern world that led to the fracture of the moral order. First, there was the shift of the primary unit of morality from the family to the individual. Just as mechanism broke the physical world down into its smallest parts, the family and society are broken down into its smallest parts: individual people. "There are, after all, no objective ideas, no moral relationships, no longer any fixed orders that hold together and organize these elements."[20] People do not naturally belong together but are forced together by necessity or circumstance.

Instead of the family being the primary unit of society, the individual is.

Second, we began to see ourselves as our own lawgivers. Instead of appealing to and judging according to a morality given by God who created both the moral and physical world, we believe that we must forge or discover this morality ourselves. "The human person forms his own religion and morality, his own world-and-life view; the main thing is that he, bound to nothing but himself, might enjoy himself and give a moment of aesthetic enjoyment to others."[21] We have taken the advice of the snake and eaten the fruit, hoping to become like gods ourselves. We no longer look to God to know good and evil, for we know it ourselves. Or so we think. However, far from unifying the human race and bringing peace, this human-centric foundation of morality has simply removed God as the foundation of the moral world and replaced it with the shifting sands of human history and preference.

Some in the modern world sought to find a new solid foundation for the moral life, but that foundation could not hold all things together. However, many either turned toward determinism or relativism. Determinism abandons the moral responsibility of living actively in the world, claiming our backgrounds and circumstances determine our actions. Relativism puts the whole weight of forming morality upon the shoulders of the individual or community, crushing us under the weight.

The results are not pretty. "Naturally, with this, all moral institutions, all establishments of family and society and state, fall apart."[22] What can we do? How can a Christian worldview sew back together what is being pulled apart? As always, the solution is to take the world as it truly is — created by the Triune God. God created both the physical and the moral world. He created the laws of thermodynamics and the Ten Commandments. Because both have the same source — God — they hold together. Christian worldview calls for the recovery of God as the divine lawgiver — the one whose actions and whose will provides the firm foundation for both the moral and physical world. There is an absolute morality in this world, because the world was made by the unchanging God. That morality transcends history does not mean that it rejects history. For the amazing thing about the Christian faith is that it enfolds and redeems history, even as our God transcends it. It is to this history of salvation that we will turn in our last chapter.

CHAPTER 7
BEAUTY RESTORED
MORALITY IN A CHRISTIAN WORLDVIEW

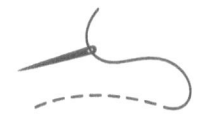

"Autonomy offered us freedom and gave us alienation. What could contingency offer us?"
- Alan Noble

"Biblically speaking, sin neither abolishes nor becomes identified with creation."
- Al Wolters

In the 1540s, Dutch artist Jan Sanders van Hemessen painted a piece known as "Christ as Triumphant Redeemer." It portrayed Jesus, with a naked torso, triumphantly displaying the wound in his side. He is not painted in agony, but, instead, demonstrating his triumph over death. The painting is bathed in a heavenly light, showing Christ as the Redeemer of the world. However, the painting was lost for centuries, as much of it had been painted over by a later artist, one with very different sensibilities (likely related both to Christ's nudity and the triumphant tone of the painting). He had darkened the painting considerably and added robes on Jesus. The second artist sought to improve the painting, but had only obscured it. In an attempt to conform Jesus (and this painting of him) to what the artist considered more suitable, he diminished and hid Jesus. When the painting was rediscovered, it had to be restored. The new paint (which was itself almost 300 years old) had to be removed so that the original beauty could be seen.[1] With the painting fully restored, we can again see this depiction of Jesus' saving victory over death.

Sometimes what is meant to improve only obscures. The modern project as a whole was intended as an improvement over the ancient and medieval world that preceded it. It sought to build every aspect of the world — including morality — on a firm and unshakeable foundation of rationality and the human self. However, by beginning with a denial or rejection of God, the modern project served to obscure rather than illuminate the moral and physical world. It painted over the whole of creation, portraying a wholly different world — one where we are the lawmakers, the judges, and the rulers of history. The original painting, in all its beauty, still exists, however, even under hundreds of years of paint.

In this chapter, we will see how the Christian worldview is able to make sense of the moral world by looking at the three major events of history: Creation, Fall, and Redemption. We will see that, as Creator, God is the source of both moral and physical laws. He holds them both together. We will also see how our culture has rejected the biblical understanding of sin and how sin is actually the best explanation for what is wrong with the world. We will end by exploring the nature of history by looking at God's work of redemption in history.

LAW AND THE LAWGIVER

In the beginning, God created the heavens and the earth (Gen 1:1). He spoke and separated light and darkness, day and night. At God's command, the seas formed and the land jutted forth. At God's instruction, the stars were put into the sky and the sun and moon were set into orbit. By the power of God's voice, life sprouted forth. God made the plants with the ability to put forth seeds and produce more of their own kind. God caused living creatures to move in the water and the air and upon the land. God also gave these living beings — fish, birds, beasts, livestock, and creeping things — the calling to increase and make more of their own kind. Even human beings, when created, were given commands. "Be fruitful and multiply, and fill the earth and subdue it; and have dominion over the fish of the sea and over the birds of the air and over every living thing that moves upon the earth" (1:28). There was a difference between the commands given to the fish and birds to increase in number and the commands given to humans. Humans had the power to obey and the power to disobey.

In the same creation story, where God creates the physical world with all its laws and structures, God also gives moral and ethical commands to humans. God commands humanity to fill and rule over the other parts of creation. Unlike the commands that govern the sun and moon, these commands are ethical and require a faithful response on the part of humanity. "The wind cannot help but obey. But human beings do have responsibility: we are held to account for the way we execute God's commandments, and we are liable to punishment if we do not execute them all."[2]

In the second chapter of Genesis, God fashions the garden as *the* place for Adam and Eve, where they will grow and live out their calling as God's children and regents on earth. But included in that calling is a command, a law, "And the LORD God commanded the man, "You may freely eat of every tree of the garden; but of the tree of the knowledge of good and evil you shall not eat, for in the day that you eat of it you shall die."" (Gen 2:16-17 NRSV). Included in the original law given in the garden is the "yes" of the creation mandate and the "no" of the forbidden fruit. From the beginning God's moral commands include both the positive call to steward creation and serve God, as well as the negative command to avoid that which God has forbidden — the fruit of the tree of the knowledge of good and evil.

The opening chapters of the Bible portray God as the divine lawgiver. He not only orders the natural law — the sun and moon, the land and sea — but also the moral law — the yes and no, the eat and do not eat. The laws for the physical and moral world both originate from the same source — the voice of God. God's speech, his Word, creates the laws for our bodies and our souls. In addition, God creates Adam, but swiftly places him into a moral-covenantal relationship with Eve. It is not good for him to be alone. He is not intended to live as an isolated individual. We are meant to live in moral relationships to one another.

The first move to deny God as lawgiver and to reject our embedded relationships comes in the very next chapter. Adam and Eve trust the serpent over God and seek to be like God themselves. They reject his moral law — his command not to eat from the tree — and send humanity into a sinful spiral. Additionally, as they are confronted about their sin, they already twist personal moral responsibility into avoidant individualism. Though Adam and Eve both eat the fruit, Adam separates himself from Eve by blaming her for their sin. He stands not with her, but apart from her. He is an individual. Eve continues the pattern when she blames the serpent. But now the harmony of the moral relationships that we were created to inhabit has been broken.

We reject the physical laws of the universe to our own peril. The laws of gravity, motion, and biology still exist even if we deny them. They still govern what brings health or harm to our bodies and creation, even if we do not understand them or choose not to believe them. "Ignoring the law of creation is impossible. The law is like a spring that can be pressed down or pushed out of sight only with great effort and that continues to make its presence felt even when repressed for a long time."[3]

Rejecting the laws of creation does not make those laws untrue. The same is true with the moral law. We reject it at our own peril. The same God who created the physical laws also spoke the moral law into existence. Moral law is just as real as physical law — both are creational laws. Just as we can live for a time pretending the physical laws of the universe do not exist, we can live for a while as if God's commands for life in this world are arbitrary, changeable, or ultimately determined by us. But eventually, both creational laws will catch up to us.

For example, our society's dominant view of sex runs counter to the creational laws. Even outside of considering who can have sex with whom (and what God says about that), our society predominantly views sex in an individualized and contractual sense. We perceive sex as fundamentally about the pleasure and satisfaction of the individuals involved. The proliferation of sex manuals in books and monthly magazines illustrates this viewpoint.[4] Anything more that comes with sex, whether union or procreation or even love, is not inherent to the act, but is a choice of those involved.

This runs contrary to how God's laws speak of sex. Yes, to some degree it's about pleasure, but more fundamentally it's about union, covenantal loyalty, and the bearing of children. We see this cultural shift even more in the growing acceptance of pornography, despite the massive consequences. Anything you want, any desires you want satisfied, you can find. As long as those who participated in the filming are consenting adults, nothing is off limits.[5] The only concerns are whether those involved in the production suffered any harm and whether they consented. When the only objective of sex is the pleasure of the individual, there can be no harm in viewing.

We can run counter to God's law for only so long before we feel its pressure. If our world views pornography as a sexual all-you-can-eat buffet, then we as a society have gorged ourselves ignoring the consequences. But the growing problem of sexual addiction in young adults and the difficulty in forming real (sexual and non-sexual) relationships testifies to the damage.[6] "If "Yes, you may" (for a price) is the sexual law in a pornographic society against which we begrudgingly permit a few exceptions, "No, you may not" is the sexual law in creation, against which God has sanctioned a few beautiful exceptions."[7]

What is viewed as a tragedy in Scripture is seen as a triumph in the modern world. The rejection of God as the lawgiver and the breaking of family/society down into isolated individuals are at the heart of modernity. "Where the creation does not find its freedom in responding obediently to the Creator's norms, there it enters bondage."[8]

We have two choices: either morality comes from us and thus has no firm foundation at all, or it comes from God, which means its foundation is secure in his wisdom and will. "There is only a choice to be made between the two: the norms of true and false, of good and evil, of beautiful and ugly emerged slowly in history by evolution, but they are not absolute, and while they are true and good today, tomorrow they may be untrue and evil; or, they have absolute and immutable being, but then they are not products of history — they merit a transcendent and metaphysical character, and because they cannot float in the sky, they have their reality in God's wisdom and will."[9] The same divine wisdom that knew the world before creating it also determined the norms of our knowing, willing, and acting. The same God said, "let the earth bring forth plants" and "do not eat from the tree of the knowledge of good and evil."

The Christian worldview holds together the moral world because it takes this world as it truly is — created by God. God created the moral and physical world and placed us into moral relationships with one another. By his Word, he created the world and gave us the law by which we are to live. We know the physical laws of creation predominantly through attending to what Christians have called "the book of nature." We look out at the world God has created, study it, and see how God holds it all together. We know the moral laws of creation, however, predominantly through attending to a different book — the book of Scripture. As Al Wolters points out, "When we attempt to discern what the normative patterns of creation are, Scripture — the architect's verbal explanation of his blueprint — is our first and indispensable guide."[10] We know the moral law by studying God's Word — the Bible.

By holding together God's law and God as the lawgiver, the Christian worldview provides a firm foundation for understanding both the moral and physical world. Christianity restores the harmony between the natural and moral order — also brings unity between thinking and doing, between head and heart.[11] Morality does not rest upon the shifting sands of history, but upon the unchanging will and wisdom of God.

SIN

The Christian worldview holds together what modernity has sought to tear apart, not only by its understanding of creation and God as lawgiver, but also through its understanding of sin as the fundamental problem that must be addressed. Every culture and people asks, "What is wrong with the world? What is wrong with me?" How we answer those questions is seen most clearly in the solutions we suggest to address the wrongs of the world.

Modernity rejects God as the lawgiver and so rejects the fundamental claim that sin is religious and ethical in character. Instead, in our culture, people tend to have three different explanations for all that is wrong with the world.

First, there are those who see the fundamental problem in

the world as a lack of knowledge, the belief that people are ignorant of what is true and what is best. A lack of information, lack of training, lack of skills (job skills, coping skills, relational skills) leads to the ills we suffer. Once we have the right information and right tools, we will do the right thing. This view asserts that people are fundamentally good, but ill-equipped. Thus, the solution is education. This can involve increasing formal education, sharing the virtues of class consciousness or capitalism, or getting secret tips and knowledge from self-help or business gurus. What we need is the right information. Why are we miserable? Clearly, we don't know about the five steps to success and happiness (here — take my online course!). Why is there poverty? We need better education (vote Yes on Prop 3). Why is there famine or disease running through countries? Evidently, we don't all understand the science of medicine or the best techniques to grow food.

Though there may be some truth that ignorance contributes to the misery in the world, as an overarching explanation for all that is wrong, this explanation falls flat. Knowledge and technique are good at solving certain problems, but they cannot reach all the way down to our hearts and souls. We all have known someone who had all the right information and the best techniques and were wicked and harmful. More information did not, in itself, make that person virtuous. It often just made him or her more effective. Imagine an crab apple tree that year in and year out bore misshapen and bitter apples. The best pruning techniques could fix some problems, but it would not make it a different tree. It might produce more, but the tree would be the same.

The second explanation that our contemporary world offers is that the fundamental problem of the world is one of bad or unjust systems. In this view, the problem is structural. Our systems have been created that provide advantages to some and exploit others. Whether we are considering education, health, government, housing, or employment, the problem lies in the structures that we have in place. Our problems stem from an inequality that has been created and perpetuated by unjust systems. The solution? Dismantle the unjust structures and replace them with equitable ones.

We see this impulse in the sometimes reforming and sometimes revolutionary drive to break down the systems of patriarchy, white privilege, redlining in housing, or worker exploitation. Fundamentally, it is the conditions that surround us that foster misery and evil. They harm and limit some people while exalting others. If we can change these conditions, we can make it so that everyone can thrive. To put it in another way, the game of life seems rigged so that some people find it easy to win while others find it impossible. The only way to fix that is to change the rules, so that they are more fair and more just.

There is much to commend in this explanation. It is true that the conditions and structures around us can be and often are unjust. It's also clear that this has deep impacts on the world. Unjust systems do create incredible misery and evil in the world. Changing structures and institutions can and often do have a long-term impact, and create genuine good in the world. However, as with the lack of knowledge, seeing systems as the primary cause of what is wrong in the world ultimately comes up short. Pointing to systemic problems may be helpful in some situations, but is insufficient as an explanation of every problem. For instance, when a man chooses to have an affair, he was *impacted* by broader pressures of manhood and virility, by systems that portray a particular kind of sexual freedom and privilege that men are entitled to, by the family system he grew up with, and many other systemic factors, but ultimately this man *made a choice* to break his marriage vows. Structures and systems influence, but they do not determine moral actions. To return to the crab apple tree, we can fertilize and irrigate to improve soil conditions, or even transplant the tree to different ground. This may impact the fruit in some healthy ways, but it does not fundamentally change the tree itself.

The third explanation favored in the modern world is metaphysical. That is, what is wrong with the world is the world itself. Evil becomes attached to something in the physical world. We see this in what our culture claims must be purged or overcome. This is common in the "remixed" religions of the modern world. By life-hacking in order to transcend the limits of the human body, we make the body itself the problem. Our bodily needs become a problem to be solved instead of a gift to be received. The language of good and bad energy, of cleansing toxins from the body, indicates that there is something "wrong" in the natural world, something that needs to be overcome or purged. We need to transcend this sad and miserable world into something greater.

By seeking a world without God or, at the very least, where God is unnecessary, the modern project participates in the very sin of Eden. Adam and Eve ate the fruit, trusting the serpent's lie that they would be like God. Ironically, we only consider the modern, yet ancient, answers to the question of sin (lack of knowledge or defect in the world) because we have already committed the ethical and religious sin of Adam and Eve. Only after we have decided that we do not need God and have rejected him do we seek explanations other than sin for what is wrong with the world.

Modernity tore apart sin (as an ethical concept) and replaced it with the language of values. Humans and human actions are no longer considered in light of natural or divine law, but only in terms of personal or communal values. As Al Wolters says, "At best they will speak of "values," a term that speaks volumes about the attempt of contemporary humanity to emancipate itself from all divine imperatives."[12] Values are something we choose, whether individually or communally.

We give them to ourselves. Laws are given to us. We do not get to choose the speed limit or how much sales tax to pay. While a city or nation does form its own laws, the contention of Christianity is that if we take the world as it truly is, we must recognize that moral and physical laws are given to us. We cannot remake them. We either keep them or break them.

The Christian faith holds together what modernity has torn apart by rejecting all three of these options as final explanations of what is wrong with the world. Instead, rooted in its claim about God as the Creator and Lawgiver, the Christian faith follows Holy Scripture in saying that sin is the fundamental problem with the world. Sin is not a mere lack of knowledge or an unjust system and cannot be attached to the very substance of creation. Instead, sin is profoundly ethical and religious. Sin is a violation of the law. Because there are norms, because there are laws in the physical and moral world given by the one Divine Lawgiver, we feel the deviation from the law more painfully. The Christian faith enfolds, unifies, and moves beyond the ignorance and structural explanations of evil, while also firmly rejecting the metaphysical explanation.

For all the work that these other explanations do to understand the wrong in the world, they ultimately take sin as less than what it truly is. "There is but one view that allows sin to be what it really is and does not weaken its reality or its nature by reasoning, and that view is from Holy Scripture. Scripture does not flatter the human being but tells him what he must be according to God's law and what he has actually become through sin."[13] Sin is the rejection of God and God's law and seeking to make our own laws and live as a law unto ourselves.

The Christian faith reveals the prior unity of the ignorance and systemic explanations for evil by positing them as symptoms of sin, not as principal causes. Sin leads to wicked and twisted systems, which in turn compound and reinforce vice and sinful behavior. Sin impacts our minds and leads to ignorance and falsehood, which enable greater wickedness. However, the root cause of both is sin, which means the complete solution is salvation. Think again about the apple tree. Bavinck claims that by recognizing the depth of sin, we are able to see how deep and necessary salvation is. "If a tree shall bring forth good fruit, then it must first be made good."[14]

If we do not know salvation as a work of God, we must either truly recognize sin for what it is and be in despair or we must minimize the serious character of sin in order to make salvation possible. "Once again, it is the Christian religion alone that reconciles the antinomy, that fully recognizes the moral decay and inability of human nature and yet opens to us a way of salvation. The salvation known by it, though, is not a human act but is only the work of God."[15] Only when we take the problem of sin with full seriousness as *the* problem with the world are we able to fully grasp the work of God in redemption.

SALVATION/RE-CREATION

Christianity is not a repudiation but the redemption of history. Morality does not rest upon the shifting sands of history, but upon the unchanging wisdom and will of God. However, this does not mean that Christianity has no place for history, remaining locked in a timeless world of ideals. In fact, the Christian faith can more adequately understand the place of history in the world because the work of God in creation and redemption takes place in history. "This same divine wisdom that created the world also re-creates it, and this same divine energy that makes things that exist persist also leads them to a firmly established conclusion. The plan for salvation is sealed within the plan for creation."[16] God creates and re-creates. His mighty acts occur in history. God's calling of Abraham was a historical event. God led his people out of Egypt and cast them into exile at particular moments in time. God the Son took on flesh and was born as the man Jesus Christ of the Virgin Mary in space and time. The history of God's dealings with his people, his promises and warnings, his revelation is just that — a history.

Christianity claims that the movements of history have both a beginning and an end, a start and a finish. They began with God's work of creation and will end with the final work of re-creation. We currently live during a time where sin has twisted and distorted what God has made, but we also live in a history where God does not abandon this creation, but reclaims and redeems it. Salvation in Jesus Christ has been accomplished. The full redemption of the world has been inaugurated and we await the final redemption at the return of Jesus.

Christianity is not a rejection of history or even a return to history, but the redemption of history. Salvation does not remain an idea that floats above us. Christianity is not exclusively a teaching *about* salvation, but is salvation itself, brought about by God in the history of the world. "The religion that will save humanity from sin and bring it into mastery of the good must be "history"; it must exist in a series of divine acts that carry on from the beginning to the end of history."[17] God's actions in history restore the world and restore history itself. The same God who creates the world re-creates it. "In Christianity, however, salvation is unleashed, on the one hand, on the whole cosmic process, and on the other, on the heart and soul, the core and essence of all world history. Here revelation begins in Eden, carries on through the centuries, receives its center in the person and work of Christ, and concludes with the end of the ages."[18]

This re-creation is as wide as creation and as deep as the depths of the human heart. Salvation is essential for history. In fact, in Christianity, history reaches its fullest potential as the unfolding of creation, fall, and redemption throughout every nook and cranny of the cosmos. Or, perhaps more provocatively, without Christianity there can be no true history.

History is more than simply the record of a sequence of events. Historians cannot name every single action or occurrence in a given day, let alone a year or era. They must choose what is relevant and leave aside what is not. They must trace connections between events and show their influence upon one another. Historians must deal with causes far more complex than those of chemistry or physics, because they deal with the human person. The human will, human reason, and human conscience acting in history make the causes of history far more complex and mysterious. Yet, the historian connects social, moral, physical, psychological, economic, legal, and environmental causes together to attempt to make sense of the sequences of events and their relationship to one another. Historians also, implicitly or explicitly, detail how these events brought about or undermined the good, the true, and the beautiful as they understand it. The work of the historian requires believing that events, causes, and the world itself hold together in a coherent fashion and develop in certain ways.

However, the belief that history is both development and progress stems from and only makes sense in the context of the Christian claim of God's redemption and re-creation of the world. As with science and nature, for there to be progress in history, there must be something toward which history is progressing. For history to have meaning, for it to convey progress and development, something must hold events together. There must be some end goal toward which history progresses, and there must be some way of making sense of the disparate events. "Christianity is not hostile to "history," but is the animating idea, the leading thought, the all-pervasive leaven, in it. [Christianity] gives it content and form, meaning and goal."[19]

Modernity sought to pull apart faith and history. We can see this particularly in the treatment of the person of Jesus. In the 19th century, as historians began to turn their skills toward examining the Bible (and the Gospels in particular), there began to be a divide between what scholars called "the Christ of Faith" and the "Jesus of History." The basic claim was that the "true, historical Jesus" being discovered through textual and archaeological research did not match the Christ proclaimed from the pulpits in the churches. Thus, in order not to undermine people's faith, it was necessary to separate faith from history. Doctrine and faith were relegated to the realm of values and piety and removed from the realm of objective fact and history.

There were many problems with these so-called "Quests for the Historical Jesus." The Jesus 'discovered' by these historians often looked more like the historian than like the Jesus of the Bible — reflecting the historian's values, prejudices, and social location. These quests often began with a series of anti-supernatural assumptions that ruled out miracles and Jesus' divinity before the investigation began. Even when undertaken in relatively good faith, these quests began with a suspicion and mistrust of what was given in the texts of Scripture and sought to go behind it to find the truth.

Perhaps most devastatingly, those who divided faith from history undermined many faithful Christian's confidence in history. History was seen as being on the side of the modernist, not the disciple of Jesus. They granted authority over the realm of history to those who methodologically (or personally) rejected God as the Creator and Redeemer of the world. However, there is no competition between faith and history. They fit together. "Just as the fundamental ideas of the Christian faith are supported by science and nature, they are much more so by history."[20] Not only will the study of history support the claims of the Christian faith, but the study of history is upheld and supported by the Christian faith. "Apart from and without Christianity there is no possibility of history in the proper sense, no history of the world and of humanity."[21]

CONCLUSION

Behind all the layers of paint on "Christ as Triumphant Redeemer" was the original, beautiful painting. Though a second artist had darkened and obscured the painting, underneath there remained a masterpiece. Underneath the darkening paint of the contemporary world is the world as it actually is — created and redeemed by God. The Christian worldview is not a call to a past age, but an invitation to return to the world as it truly is, and to live and believe accordingly.

Science can only stand if the Christian worldview is correct. Nature comes into its own only as the Scriptures make it known to us. History is only true history if God enters into it, creating and re-creating, and then lifting history and creation to its heights in the kingdom of heaven. We saw in this chapter how our modern world painted over God as creator and lawgiver in favor of humanity creating its own laws of morality. However, humanity is a shaky foundation. Only God can hold together and hold up both the moral and physical laws of the world.

We also saw how, in rejecting God as lawgiver, our culture has moved away from the concept of sin as the explanation for what is wrong with the world (and us). Instead, it has settled for a variety of lesser, unsatisfactory explanations. By recovering sin as a violation of God's law, the Christian worldview holds together the truth found in these lesser explanations as it subsumes them under sin as lawlessness. Lastly, we saw that when history is disconnected from the beginning of all things in creation and the end of all things in the kingdom of God, it is not able to be true history. We are able to hold together the various events of human history and see them progressing toward a goal only because God created and redeems the world.

Beneath the layers of paint obscuring the world God made is something that is good, true, and beautiful. Underneath is the beauty of God's law, God's wisdom, and God's way. Underneath is the truth of our fall into sin and the world's fall along with us. Underneath is the goodness of God's salvation. Even when we cannot see it clearly, the masterpiece is there.

CONCLUSION
ON LIVING IN A FRACTURED WORLD

> *"Just as the wisdom of God became flesh in Christ,
> so should the truth also enter us."*
> - Herman Bavinck

> *"Lift up your hearts. We lift them up unto the Lord"*
> - Great Prayer of Thanksgiving

How did we get here? We have spent the last seven chapters analyzing the cultural, technological, and intellectual shifts that have led to the frantic fractures of our present age. We have also traced an alternative to the common vision of ourselves and the world around us.

Where do we go from here? This is a far more difficult question to answer. The Christian worldview we have sketched in this book is like a train running down the tracks. Everyone else believes there is only one train, and they are not worried about the destination, because it is the only train running. When we begin to inhabit a Christian worldview in our thinking, our loving, and our practices, it will be like jumping onto a different train. Those around us may not have even heard of the train and, if they have, they don't believe it is running anymore. But you tell them, "this train runs fine, better even than the one you are on."

Even if we begin to acknowledge a different (and better) train on the tracks, it is difficult to switch trains while they are in motion. The modern project is so deeply ingrained in our culture and our institutions that there will need to be significant crisis and collapse for people to begin to look for alternatives.

As we seek to answer the question, "Where do we go from here?," we must see a Christian worldview not as an intellectual accomplishment, but as a gift and an obligation to pursue. We will look at two potential first steps forward in seeking to live a Christian worldview, but before we do, we must draw the diagnosis of our times to a close.

THE MODERN PROBLEM

The modern project is rooted in discontentment. We tend to seek something new because of our discontentment with things as they are. As Bavinck notes, "it is noticeable everywhere and in each domain that there is a great dissatisfaction with what exists."[1] We see this in the religiously remixed who are not content with the institutional religions that already exist. We see this in the technological push to move beyond our limits. We see this in the rejection of moral laws in favor of personal value statements. We see this in the widespread discontent with the status quo. Everyone, everywhere admits that things are not the way we want them to be.

At times, Christians share in this discontent and at times they cannot. God's good creation has been twisted by sin and this shows up in wicked systems, unjust laws, exploitation, and more. When this happens, Christians stand with even greater confidence against such evil because we know the Creator, know who we are and know what this world was made for. We can see evil more clearly for what it is because, in Christ, we have a clearer vision of the good from which evil has departed. However, when it comes to what is given us in creation — creaturely limits, the moral law, or the structure of the physical world — as Christians, we cannot join in the discontent. Instead, we see in this form of discontent a desire to be like God, a desire as old as the exile from Eden. At the core of modern mistrust is the belief that God (and the Christian faith) cannot provide an adequate foundation for viewing the world.

Modernity is seen not only in discontent, but in its particular response to discontent. Every age has individuals dissatisfied with the status quo, and often for good reason. However, modernity's response to this feeling is to reject God and go back to the beginning, to break things down into their most basic parts. Modernity attempts to start over, to dig down to the bedrock of human knowledge, civilization, and morality and to build a whole new structure on a firmer foundation. God is not a firm enough foundation, so we must go deeper to find something with which no one can possibly disagree. So modernity seeks "to go back to the last elements, to the original components, to the so-called positive, indisputable facts."[2] In knowledge, we go back to the simplest perceptions, the most basic thoughts. In nature, we break everything down into atoms or energies. In the family, society, and state, we must go down to the individual. Modernity is not content to find the basic building blocks, but to build a new world on these foundations. Whatever direction or form these impulses take, there is "the aspiration to build a new, better world from these original elements."[3]

As we have seen, these basic building blocks do not end up being strong enough to hold the weight they have been asked to bear. It is as if we have asked the branches to carry what the trunk of the tree was made to bear. The branches eventually break under that weight. Ultimately, only God can serve as the foundation of our understanding of the world, of ourselves, and of our place in it.

At its heart, modernity is a search for autonomy ("self-rule"). It is a rejection of God as the lawgiver and humans as bound by external laws. We would make the laws for ourselves. We would find the foundations and we would build on our own. In searching for autonomy, we got anarchy ("lawlessness"). The chaos and all the forms of fracture we live with today are symptoms of the basic desire to be our own rulers and our own gods. Bavinck rightly sees a rejection of radical autonomy and a return to dependence upon God in every sphere of life as a fundamental characteristic of the Christian worldview.

> "It is this autonomy and anarchy that the Christian worldview resists with all its strength. According to it, the human being is not autonomous but is always and everywhere bound to laws that were not devised by him but that are prescribed to him by God as the rule of his life. In religion and morality, in science and art, in family, society, and state, ideas are everywhere, norms above him, which mutually form a unity and have their origin and existence in the Creator and Lawgiver of the universe."[4]

We live in a world made by God. We cannot conform it to ourselves, but we must be conformed to it. The moral and physical laws of the universe exist independent of us, and we ignore them to our own peril. The challenge of early ages was *which* authority to trust. The challenge of our present age is *whether* we will acknowledge any authority at all. "In maintaining the objectivity of God's word and law, all Christians are agreed and should stand together unanimously. The battle today is no longer about the authority of pope or council, of church and confession; for countless others it is no longer even about the authority of " or the person of Christ. The question on the agenda asks, as principally as possible, whether there is still some authority and some law to which the human person is bound."[5]

CHRISTIAN WORLDVIEW: A GIFT AND AN OBLIGATION

The modern pursuit of autonomy has made life seem frayed at the seams. Our goal in recovering Christian worldview is to mend what modernity has torn. It is to present a vision for the whole of life, the whole of human knowledge, and the whole of the world as it truly is, created by and dependent upon God the Creator.

To return to the image with which we began this book, worldview is a needle. It is meant to sew together what has ripped apart, not to puncture holes in other people and their positions. We have looked at this breakdown of a unified worldview in the realms of knowledge, nature, and morality. We have also looked at how recovering a Christian worldview shows the prior unity behind the present fractures.

But what now? With all the forces shaping and disciplining us throughout the week, can we truly recover a Christian worldview in our churches? Can we even recover a Christian worldview individually, let alone as a broader Western culture?

This brings us back to James K. A. Smith's critique of Christian worldview. Discipleship — and Christian worldview as a part of discipleship — is not an intellectual achievement. It is not a tool for winning an argument with your nephew at Thanksgiving. The heart must be shaped as well as the mind, which requires much more than new information. If recovering a Christian worldview was only a matter of getting all the right ideas in our heads, it would have happened a long time ago. It would be great if we could solve all the ills of our society, the church, and our lives simply by thinking correctly about a

Christian worldview. Yet, as Alan Noble acknowledges, it is much harder than that. "If everyone in America suddenly acknowledged that they are not their own but belong to God, we would still be left with systems, institutions, practices, and tools that are designed for the sovereign self, and it wouldn't take long before we found ourselves right back where we started."[6]

Living this unified worldview is hard, lifelong work, particularly with so many cross-pressures in our world. In the Belhar Confession, the unity of the body of Christ, the church, is described in this way:

> "[U]nity is, therefore, both a gift and an obligation for the church of Jesus Christ; that through the working of God"s Spirit it is a binding force, yet simultaneously a reality which must be earnestly pursued and sought: one which the people of God must continually be built up to attain.[7]"

The unity of the church is both a gift and an obligation. It is a gift because the unity of the church is accomplished through Christ's work of reconciliation. We *are* united because we are one in Christ Jesus. Yet, the gift of unity calls for a response from us. It calls for us to make it visible in how we live together as Christ's body. It is "a reality which must be earnestly pursued and sought."

Something similar can be said about a Christian worldview. The world itself is an organic unity, filled with diversity, governed by God's unchanging wisdom, and headed toward the goal of the kingdom of God. This is true because God created the world, rules it, and is re-creating it. In this way, the Christian worldview is a gift because it already exists because of the wonderful work of God.

Yet, simultaneously, the Christian worldview is a reality we must seek and pursue. It is true, but this truth must be made visible in our life together as God's people and our life in the world.

This side of the Fall, there has never been a time where we could say that the culture was completely in line with a Christian worldview. This vision of the world has always existed as both a gift and an obligation. This does not set aside our responsibility in pursuing it or in working to make it visible in our churches, our lives, and our culture. But pursuing a Christian worldview is the work of more than one lifetime. Though we may only make a beginning, let's look at two potential first steps in pursuing a Christian worldview: reformation and worship.

PURSUE REFORMATION OVER REVOLUTION

What does renewal look like in our world and in our lives? It looks more like reform than revolution. Reform is the slow work of receiving what is good with gratitude while rejecting what is bad. Revolution is the radical work of cutting everything back to the roots and starting over. Reform acknowledges that nothing is perfectly evil or perfectly good in this fallen world. There is always good to be received even as there is a need for renewal, for a new direction, for errors to be rejected and removed. Revolution is impatient with imperfection and partial progress. It wants all or nothing. Reform is willing to take small victories and put up with much that is far from perfect. As Al Wolters says, "This sanctification is *progressive renewal* rather than *violent overthrow*."[8]

Pursuing a Christian worldview along the path of reform rather than revolution can be seen in how we view renewal and sanctification in our own life. We expect slow, patient progress as we grow in Christ. We reject the impatience that requires us to be fully holy right now or else we are worthless. This is where habits and practices are of immense value. As rituals that form our hearts by directing our bodies, our thoughts, and our mouths, holy habits can be an instrument through which God slowly sanctifies us. He redirects our hearts to seek Christ and his Kingdom.

Pursuing a Christian worldview through reform is also seen in how sanctification takes place in the church. Every church is flawed and in need of renewal. The healthiest and fastest growing church has distortions and sins that need to be addressed. But even sick and dwindling churches can also have good that should be received. "We ought not to respond to a sick church by rejecting it wholesale or by refusing to participate in its life, but by attaching ourselves to and building on the good that can still be found in it."[9] The outward success of a church (or lack thereof) does not excuse the sins or toxicity that may exist within it. But the smallness and troubles of a church does not mean there is nothing good in it. Pursuing a Christian worldview along the path of reform will help us be sober-minded about whatever congregation we belong to. We neither expect perfection, nor excuse wickedness.

Reform is even seen in how sanctification is seen in the culture. It is the spirit of revolution that chooses brash moves or scorched earth tactics in order to "take back the culture for God." The spirit of reform is genuinely active, but in humble and small ways. In pursuing Christian worldview, we will reject revolution, but also quietism. There is always some good to be received, but also always some distortion to be renewed. "As a result some element in every situation is worth preserving. Conversely, everything in reality falls within the scope of religious direction: everything that exists is susceptible to sinful distortion and is in need of religious renewal."[10] This will be as true in politics, education, agriculture, urban planning, waste removal, information technology, and social work as it is in the church.

In short, pursuing Christian worldview will require that we

not be content with things as they are, but that we also receive this world (and even much of what humans have made in it) as a gift from God. As Paul tells us in 1 Thessalonians 5:21b-22, "hold on to what is good, reject every kind of evil."

SURSUM CORDA

Ultimately, pursuing a Christian worldview is about pursuing God. It is not simply thinking correct thoughts about God, but living life before the face of God. It is receiving this world God has made with gratitude and living well in it. The goal of pursuing a Christian worldview is caught up in the goal of all discipleship: to love the Lord our God with all our heart, soul, mind, and strength and to love our neighbor as ourselves.

In worship, we come before the living God. In worship, we lift up our hearts to the Lord (sursum corda). We gather in God's presence as God's people in the sanctuary. This is a beautiful privilege. However, it is not only when we are singing, praying, listening, eating, drinking, or washing in worship that we live before the face of God. All of the Christian life is lived before the face of God. Worship shapes and disciples our hearts to live all of life in God's presence. Thus, if we are going to inhabit well a Christian worldview, if we are going to receive the world as it truly is and live well in it before the face of God, then we must attend well to our worship. As James K. A. Smith says, "So if we want to discern the shape of a Christian worldview, it is crucial that we recall the priority of liturgy to doctrine. Doctrines, beliefs, and a Christian worldview emerge *from* the nexus of Christian worship practices; worship is the *matrix* of Christian faith, not its "expression" or "illustration.""[11] We need worship if we want worldview.

Having come before God's presence in worship, we are then called to live the whole of our lives before the face of God — at home, at work, at the store, when in the company of others, when we are alone, when we are online, and when we are offline. Bavinck sees this emphasis clearly in the writings of the Reformer John Calvin, who called us to receive creation as the theater of God's glory. Bavinck says,

> "Again and again, Calvin's writings include the phrase *coram Deo*, 'in God's presence.' He sets all things, the whole world and in particular humanity, directly in relation to God and placed before his countenance. He examines everything in light of eternity and throws a glimpse of divine glory to the creation. The whole world, in all its length and breadth, is so to be viewed; as an organic and harmonious whole, between God's design and final goal, for which he intended his creation. It is an instrument, an organ, a musical instrument in his hand, and that for the honor of his name."[12]

The world is a musical instrument in the hands of God. When we regularly and intentionally gather in worship, we learn to hear the tune he is playing.

CONCLUSION

Pursuing a Christian worldview is ultimately about pursuing God. God created the world in all its fullness and created us to live in it. There is a fittingness to our life in the world. However, it is a fittingness we find only when we live trusting in God. When we see God at the center, we can make sense of how we know the world around us. When we see God the Creator and his unchanging wisdom, we can make sense of this stable and changing world so full of life. When we see God the Lawgiver, we can make sense of how to receive this world we have made and to walk well with God and others in it. Indeed, in him all things hold together.

Bavinck ends *Christian Worldview* with a call to a more

humble, more confident, and more beautiful embodiment of the Christian faith. This is a fitting end to our pursuit of a Christian worldview as well. For the Christian religion is

> "to serve God with all your mind, with all your soul, and with all your might, to make oneself a living, holy sacrifice pleasing to God; it is to trust unconditionally in God as the rock of salvation and of our portion in eternity. The truth is objective; it exists independently of us. It does not direct itself toward us; we have to direct ourselves toward it. But just as the wisdom of God became flesh in Christ, so should the truth also enter us. In the path of freedom, it must become our personal and spiritual property; through a living and true faith, it must become constitutive of our thinking and doing and then spread outside us until the earth is full of the knowledge of the Lord."[13]

ENDNOTES

INTRODUCTION

1. Albert M. Wolters, *Creation Regained: Biblical Basics for a Reformational Worldview*, Second Edition (Grand Rapids, MI: Eerdmans, 2005), 2.
2. Wolters, *Creation Regained*, 2. The following paragraph draws from Wolter's own explication of his definition on pages 2-3.
3. James K. A. Smith, *Desiring the Kingdom: Worship, Worldview, and Cultural Formation* (Grand Rapids, MI: Baker Academic, 2009), 40-46
4. Smith, *Desiring the Kingdom*, 47.
5. Smith, *Desiring the Kingdom*, 42-43.
6. Smith, *Desiring the Kingdom*, 64.
7. Smith, *Desiring the Kingdom*, 138.
8. I explore some of these formative practices more deeply in another book, *Rooted: Growing in Christ in a Rootless Age* (Brantford, Ontario: Peniel Press, 2022).
9. Herman Bavinck, *Christian Worldview*, trans. and ed. Nathaniel Gray Sutanto, James Eglinton, and Cory C. Brock (Wheaton, IL: Crossway, 2019), 110.

1. MADE TO MEND

1. Bavinck, *Christian Worldview*, 21-22.
2. Ibid., 22.
3. Alan Noble, *You Are Not Your Own: Belonging to God in an Inhuman World* (Downer's Grove, IL: Intervarsity Press, 2021), 71.
4. Noble, *You Are Not Your Own*, 1.
5. Augustine, City of God, Translated by Henry Bettenson. Penguin Books: London, 1972. XIX.24, p 890.

    I owe this connection to our current culture to a conversation on Augustine's City of God with Graham Shearer, Duncan Hollands, Sarah Pike, and Iulia Miaun.
6. Bavinck, *Christian Worldview*, 23.
7. Tara Isabella Burton, *Strange Rites: New Religions for a Godless World* (New York: Public Affairs, 2020), 23.
8. Burton, 23.
9. Burton, 22

10. Burton, 25.
11. Bavinck, *Christian Worldview*, 24.
12. Bavinck, *Christian Worldview*, 26.
13. Bavinck, *Christian Worldview*, 25-26.
14. Bavinck, *Christian Worldview*, 27.
15. Bavinck, *Christian Worldview*, 28.
16. Bavinck, *Christian Worldview*, 28.
17. It is important to note that this is a metaphysical claim, not a historical one. The reality (or unreality) of Christendom, the ascendency or waning of the Christian faith, has nothing to do with this claim.
18. Noble, *You Are Not Your Own*, 11.
19. Noble, *You Are Not Your Own*, 3.
20. Bavinck, *Christian Worldview*, 27.
21. Noble, *You Are Not Your Own*, 90.

2. FLYING HALF A SHIP

1. *Star Wars, Episode III: Revenge of the Sith*
2. Bavinck, *Christian Worldview*, 32.
3. Bavinck, *Christian Worldview*, 32.
4. Bavinck, *Christian Worldview*, 40-41.
5. Though this quotation is commonly attributed to Mark Twain, I cannot find the exact quote. The closest is in Tom Sawyer Abroad (1894), where it says, "But, on the other hand, Uncle Abner said that the person that had took a bull by the tail once had learnt sixty or seventy times as much as a person that hadn't, and said a person that started in to carry a cat home by the tail was gitting knowledge that was always going to be useful to him, and warn't ever
    going to grow dim or doubtful."
6. Burton, *Strange Rites*, 184.
7. Burton, 185.
8. Rene Descartes, "Fifth Meditation" and "Sixth Meditation" in *Meditations on the First Philosophy in Which the Existence of God and the Real Distinction between the Soul and the Body or Man are Demonstrated*. 1641.
9. However, for much of postmodern philosophy, Descartes was not seen as radical enough.
10. Burton, 190.
11. Chip Heath and Dan Heath, *Switch: How to Change Things When Change is Hard* (New York: Broadway Books, 2010), 7.
12. Burton, 190.
13. Bavinck, *Christian Worldview*, 32.
14. Bavinck, *Christian Worldview*, 33.

15. James K. A. Smith, *How (Not) to be Secular: Reading Charles Taylor* (Grand Rapids, MI: Eerdmans, 2014), 99.
16. Alan Noble, *Disruptive Witness: Speaking Truth in a Distracted Age* (Downer's Grove, IL: Intervarsity Press, 2018), 45.
17. Noble, *Disruptive Witness,* 48.
18. Noble, *Disruptive Witness,* 49.
19. In detailing Charles Taylor's taxonomy, I am drawing primarily from James K. A. Smith's "How Not to be Secular" 20-22.
20. Smith, *How (Not) to be Secular,* 21-22.
21. Smith, *How (Not) to be Secular,* 63.
22. Bavinck, *Christian Worldview,* 37.
23. Bavinck, *Christian Worldview,* 36.
24. Bavinck, *Christian Worldview,* 37.
25. Bavinck, *Christian Worldview,* 38.
26. Bavinck, *Christian Worldview,* 38.
27. Wolters, *Creation Regained,* 33.
28. Bavinck, *Christian Worldview,* 47
29. Bavinck, *Christian Worldview,* 47

3. IT ALL DEPENDS (ON GOD)

1. Bavinck, *Christian Worldview,* 37.
2. Wolters, *Creation Regained,* 27.
3. Bavinck rightly makes the caveat that we can have our experience of sensation and/or representation be the actual object of knowledge, but only when being intentionally self-reflective. This is not the normal way of considering our experience. Bavinck, *Christian Worldview,* 36.
4. Bavinck, *Christian Worldview,* 36.
5. Bavinck, *Christian Worldview,* 46.
6. Wolters, 28.
7. Bavinck, *Christian Worldview,* 45.
8. Bavinck, *Christian Worldview,* 46.
9. Bavinck, *Christian Worldview,* 46.
10. Bavinck, *Christian Worldview,* 43.
11. Wolters, 36.
12. James K. A. Smith, *Who's Afraid of Relativism: Community, Contingency, and Creaturehood* (Grand Rapids, MI: Baker Books, 2014), 50.
13. Bavinck, *Christian Worldview,* 34.
14. Alan Jacobs, *How to Think: A Survival Guide for a World at Odds* (New York: Currency, 2017), 16.
15. Jacobs, 43.
16. Smith, *Who's Afraid of Relativism,* 31.

17. This initial posture often leads to a "God of the gaps" theism, where God is used as the explanation for the unexplainable. Where there are gaps in our knowledge, we can appeal to God, but where our knowledge seems secure, God is cut out of the equation. As many have pointed out, the apparent increase of our knowledge of the physical world would then appear to make God smaller, or at least, more and more irrelevant. For many of the founders of modernity (and particularly the Enlightenment), this is precisely the point.
18. Bavinck, *Christian Worldview*, 47.
19. John Webster, *Holiness* (Grand Rapids, MI: Eerdmans, 2003), 10.
20. Webster, 11.
21. Webster, 11.
22. Webster, 15.
23. Webster, 23.
24. Webster, 25.

4. LIFE FINDS A WAY

1. Bavinck, *Christian Worldview*, 61-62.
2. Bavinck, *Christian Worldview*, 58.
3. Noble, *You Are Not Your Own*, 55.
4. Noble, *You Are Not Your Own*, 54.
5. Noble notes that both the left and the right use the language of efficiency when they make arguments for public policy. Not only what we argue for is shaped by our obsession for efficiency, but the very arguments that we find convincing (or not) are shaped by it. See Noble, *You Are Not Your Own*, 54-55.
6. Smith, *How (Not) to be Secular*, 64.
7. Steven Spielberg. *Jurassic Park*. United States: Universal Pictures, 1993.
8. Bavinck, *Christian Worldview*, 60.
9. William Shakespeare, Hamlet, Act I, Scene V.
10. Burton, *Strange Rites*, 98.
11. Burton, 98.
12. Burton, 98. The Jakki Smith-Leonardini quote comes from "Clearing Out Old Energy," Goop, https://goop.com/wellness/spirituality/clearing-out-old-energy/
13. Hylozoism and Panpsychism respectively, see Bavinck, *Christian Worldview*, 63.
14. Burton, 99.
15. Bavinck, *Christian Worldview*, 61.
16. Smith, *How (Not) to be Secular*, 70-71.
17. Bavinck, *Christian Worldview*, 69.

18. This is not to dismiss the importance of the scientific or philosophical arguments, but only to say that we can make all of those and yet miss what is truly driving the contemporary growth of this belief.
19. Because much of contemporary dynamism is pantheism and/or heterodox theologically, much of it is not interested in the God of Scripture, but in a generic 'god.' Hence the lack of capitalization in this sentence.
20. Some Darwinian thinking will seek to find some purpose in change/adaptation by claiming 'survival' as the sole purpose of life, but this explanation falls far short of what is meant when we talk about what something is *for*. What is survival for? If every adaptation is to increase the survival of the species, what is the purpose of the species survival? Is there anything greater than life itself? What about art or music? How do they increase the survival of the species?
21. Bavinck, *Christian Worldview,* 67.
22. Bavinck, *Christian Worldview,* 67-68.
23. Bavinck, *Christian Worldview,* 72-73.
24. Bavinck, *Christian Worldview,* 73.
25. Bavinck, *Christian Worldview,* 66-67.

5. CERTIFIED ORGANIC

1. Bavinck, *Christian Worldview,* 72.
2. James Eglinton, *Trinity and Organism: Towards a New Reading of Herman Bavinck's Organic Motif.* T&T Clark Studies in Systematic Theology, Volume 17. (London: Bloomsbury T&T Clark, 2012), 67.
3. Herman Bavinck, *Reformed Dogmatics, Volume 2: God and Creation*, edited by John Bolt, translated by John Vriend (Grand Rapids: Baker Academic, 2004), 435-436.
4. Eglinton, 67.
5. Eglinton, 67.
6. Eglinton, 70.
7. Eglinton, 72.
8. Eglinton, 68.
9. Part of Eglinton's project is rightly to differentiate Bavinck's organicism from Idealist organicism on the basis of Bavinck's own claims about his position.
10. Eglinton, 69.
11. Elginton, 69
12. Bavinck, *Christian Worldview,* 57.
13. Eglinton, 69.
14. Eglinton, 69.
15. Westminster Shorter Catechism, Question 1.

16. Bavinck, *Christian Worldview*, 73.
17. Bavinck, *Christian Worldview*, 77-78.
18. Wolters, 31.
19. Bavinck, *Christian Worldview*, 80.
20. Bavinck, *Christian Worldview*, 75-76. Based upon correspondence with Al Wolters, I have chosen to translate the Dutch *leest* as "gather" rather than "perceive" as it is an allusion to Matthew 7:16.
21. Smith, *How (Not) to be Secular*, 41.
22. Bavinck, *Christian Worldview*, 81-82.
23. Smith, *How (Not) to be Secular*, 42.
24. Bavinck, *Christian Worldview*, 83.
25. Smith, *Desiring the Kingdom*, 143.
26. Noble, *You Are Not Your Own*, 130.
27. Wolters, 59.

6. NO FOUNDATION

1. Immanuel Kant, *"What is Enlightenment?"*, translated by Mary C. Smith http://www.columbia.edu/acis/ets/CCREAD/etscc/kant.html
2. Kant, *"What is Enlightenment?"*
3. Bavinck, *Christian Worldview*, 102-103.
4. Bavinck, *Christian Worldview*, 94.
5. Bavinck, *Christian Worldview*, 95.
6. Smith, *How (Not) to be Secular*, 107.
7. Smith, *How (Not) to be Secular*, 107.
8. Wolters, *Creation Regained*, 50.
9. Wolters, 61.
10. Bavinck, *Christian Worldview*, 100.
11. Bavinck, *Christian Worldview*, 102.
12. Smith, *Who's Afraid of Relativism*, 21.
13. Noble, *You Are Not Your Own*, 21.
14. Noble, *You Are Not Your Own*, 70.
15. Noble, *You Are Not Your Own*, 27.
16. Noble, *You Are Not Your Own*, 25.
17. Bavinck, *Christian Worldview*, 100.
18. Noble, *You Are Not Your Own*, 30-31.
19. Noble, *You Are Not Your Own*, 31.
20. Bavinck, *Christian Worldview*, 103.
21. Bavinck, *Christian Worldview*, 102.
22. Bavinck, *Christian Worldview*, 102.

7. BEAUTY RESTORED

1. https://www.sothebys.com/en/auctions/ecatalogue/2019/master-paintings-evening-n10007/lot.17.html
2. Wolters, *Creation Regained*, 17.
3. Wolters, 62.
4. The popular argument for rejecting abstinence prior to marriage because of 'sexual compatibility' is another symptom of this change. "What if the sex is bad?" they say. But what if, instead, the amount of dopamine produced is not the only definition of good and if the quality of sex is not the foundation for a successful relationship?
5. The rise of sex robots and advanced CG is testing even these few limits in our society. If no actual people were involved in the sex act, then "no one was harmed" in making the pornography.
6. There are numerous articles and studies on the negative impact of pornography on relationships, including:
    https://extension.usu.edu/relationships/research/effects-of-pornography-on-relationships
    https://www.npr.org/2017/10/09/556606108/research-explores-the-effect-pornography-has-on-long-term-relationships
7. Noble, *You Are Not Your Own*, 148.
8. Wolters, 66.
9. Bavinck, *Christian Worldview*, 108.
10. Wolters, 109.
11. Bavinck, *Christian Worldview*, 110.
12. Wolters, 17.
13. Bavinck, *Christian Worldview*, 111.
14. Bavinck, *Christian Worldview*, 112.
15. Bavinck, *Christian Worldview*, 113.
16. Bavinck, *Christian Worldview*, 113-114.
17. Bavinck, *Christian Worldview*, 115.
18. Bavinck, *Christian Worldview*, 115-116.
19. Bavinck, *Christian Worldview*, 121.
20. Bavinck, *Christian Worldview*, 120.
21. Bavinck, *Christian Worldview*, 120.

CONCLUSION

1. Bavinck, *Christian Worldview*, 126.
2. Bavinck, *Christian Worldview*, 126.
3. Bavinck, *Christian Worldview*, 127.
4. Bavinck, *Christian Worldview*, 128
5. Bavinck, *Christian Worldview*, 129

6. Noble, *You Are Not Your Own*, 161.
7. The Belhar Confession, Article 2 in *Our Faith: Ecumenical Creed, Reformed Confessions, and Other Resources* (Grand Rapids, MI: Faith Alive, 2013), 146.
8. Wolters, 91.
9. Wolters, 95.
10. Wolters, 93.
11. Smith, *Desiring the Kingdom*, 138.
12. Herman Bavinck, *Johannes Calvijn* (Kampen: J. H. Kok, 1909), 17-18. Cited in Eglinton, *Trinity and Organism*, 77.
13. Bavinck, *Christian Worldview*, 132.

ACKNOWLEDGMENTS

Though my name sits on the cover, there are many people who worked behind the scenes to make this book what it has become. All errors and mistakes are my own, but much that was in this book become better because of them. I thank God for each of them.

To Bethel Reformed Church, whose love for the Word of God and for me, their pastor, never ceases to astound me.

To Brantford Christian School, for embodying what it means to teach and live a Christian worldview, and for partnering with my family in shaping my children to see how in Christ all things hold together.

To my mother-in-law, Anja Noordam, for reading through an early draft and providing feedback. Writing with you and Dad in mind has made me a better writer.

To my father, Tim Shaffer, for providing his copyediting and proofreading expertise to this work. Hopefully, I will eventually learn to make all my verbs and subjects agree, so that you have less work to do.

To my wife, Olga Shaffer, whose endless encouragement and love has helped me through the highs and lows of writing this book. You were excited when I was gushing about Bavinck (again) and you believed in me and this project when I was tempted to throw it all away and start over.

To my children, Elijah, Moriah, and Joanna. Thank you for your patience with a daddy who spent many a Saturday afternoon working on another book.

Also by
Stephen C. Shaffer

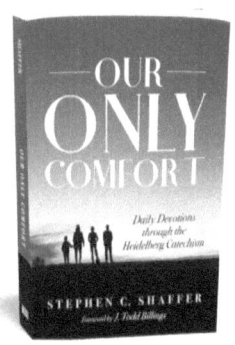

Our Only Comfort: Daily Devotions through the Heidelberg Catechism

In a fast-paced world full of distractions, how do we create space to have conversations about faith? Parents long to talk about Jesus with their children, but are unsure where to begin. Families want to slow down and reconnect with what matters most, but struggle to squeeze anything into already busy schedules. Teens and adults desire to go deeper in their faith, but are filled with unanswered questions. In *Our Only Comfort*, Rev. Stephen Shaffer provides individuals and families with a helpful structure for growing in Christian faith. In a series of 364 devotions, *Our Only Comfort* will take families, young adults, and new believers through the core teachings of the Christian faith through the lens of the Heidelberg Catechism. Wrestling through questions like "Who is Jesus?" "How do I pray?" and "What does it mean to keep the Ten Commandments?" these short devotions create opportunity for conversations about faith between parents and children and provide nourishment for faith to grow.

Paperback: 978-1725298736
Hardcover: 978-1725298743

Rooted: Growing in Christ in a Rootless Age

In a rootless world, we long for a place where we find peace, rest, and belonging.

The longing for home, for place, for rootedness is ultimately a longing for Jesus. Wrestling with the biblical themes of land and exile, *Rooted: Growing in Christ in a Rootless Age* is a call to grow more at home in our true home, Jesus Christ. Walking along with Israel from Eden through the Exodus to the Exile, Stephen C. Shaffer shows how God both rooted and uprooted his people so that they would find their identity and center in God.

Paperback: 978-1777978709
Hardcover: 978-1777978716

www.ingramcontent.com/pod-product-compliance
Lightning Source LLC
Chambersburg PA
CBHW030301100526
44590CB00012B/472